EMPOWERED: MASTER YOUR EMOTIONS IN RELATIONSHIPS

The Ultimate Handbook For Building Positive Connections In All Areas of Your Life

RACHEL STONE

Copyright © 2023 by Rachel Stone

All rights reserved.

No part of this book may be reproduced in any form or by any electronic or mechanical means, including information storage and retrieval systems, without written permission from the author, except for the use of brief quotations in a book review.

Introduction

Are you feeling like your emotions are taking control of your relationships? Do attachment issues cause you constant anxiety or stress? You're not alone. Many people, just like you, struggle with managing their emotions in relationships, leading to unhealthy connections and unnecessary strain.

But fear not! This book is here to help you.

This handbook will help you understand the importance of creating strong connections in all areas of your life, from your partner and boss to random strangers on the street. That's right: mastering emotions is crucial for successful relationships.

I will guide you through understanding emotions, such as grief, trauma, sadness, depression, envy, and jealousy; address common questions about managing emotions in relationships; dispel myths; and delve into the neuroscience behind different emotions and why they're essential for healthy connections.

I understand how challenging mastering emotions can be. There-

Introduction

fore, this handbook will give you practical examples and real-world applications.

You will gain an awareness of your thoughts, feelings, and physical sensations in the present moment without judgement or reaction.

By practising mindfulness, you will learn to observe emotions without getting overwhelmed and build greater emotional resilience and self-control. You'll gain the skills to increase your emotional intelligence, develop self-awareness and self-love, and manage emotional triggers in a healthy way.

At the end of each chapter, you'll find practical steps to guide you towards a new way of creating lasting connections, including overcoming attachment worries, developing emotional resilience, practising mindfulness in relationships, setting healthy boundaries, dealing with jealousy, and learning how to forgive and let go.

My purpose for creating this handbook is to empower you in your relationships by offering practical advice and guidance on topics such as creating healthy boundaries and dealing with attachment anxieties.

Imagine reducing anxiety, exuding confidence, and living stress-free in all your relationships - that's what this handbook will do for you.

After reading this handbook, you will feel more secure and less stressed throughout your connections, and you will have learned practical applications and concrete steps towards healthier relationships with others.

So let's begin this journey today, shall we?

1

Understanding Emotions
THE MANY DIFFERENT TYPES WE EXPERIENCE

Emotions are internal feelings that help us comprehend and interpret the world. They can range from happiness to sadness, with many types like grief, trauma, depression, envy, and jealousy.

Different emotions

Grief: When someone we love, such as a family member, dies, we experience immense sadness.

Trauma: When something frightening occurs, it can leave us deeply upset and terrified for a long time.

Sadness: When we feel unhappy or down.

Depression: People may experience intense sadness for an extended period and find it difficult to carry out daily tasks.

Envy: This emotion occurs when we desire something that someone else has.

Jealousy: When someone close to us expresses more affection for another individual than us, we might experience feelings of jealousy.

Happiness: When we feel joyful and content, it can lead to happiness. This positive emotion usually stems from positive events in our lives.

Excitement: The feeling of being eager and enthusiastic.

Love: An intense feeling of affection and care for someone or something, including family members, friends, pets, or even hobbies.

Pride: When we feel good about something we've accomplished or done, pride arises. It is a source of motivation and self-worth.

Gratitude: Gratitude is the feeling of being thankful for what we have or the kindness others show us. It helps us appreciate all of life's good things.

Relaxation: When we feel calm and at ease, relaxation occurs. This emotion often arises from taking a break or enjoying a peaceful moment.

Curiosity: When we want to learn or discover something new, it compels us to ask questions and explore the world.

Amusement: Amusement is the feeling of being entertained or finding something humorous. We may experience this emotion while watching a comedy or spending time with amusing friends.

Emotions can shape our daily lives, both positively and negatively.

Empowered: Master Your Emotions In Relationships

Understanding and managing our emotions will help us lead happier, healthier, and more rewarding lives.

2

Unlocking The Power Of Emotions
THE CRUCIAL ROLE THEY PLAY IN OUR LIVES

An emotion is a complex psychological state accompanied by physiological modifications in the body, such as changes to the heart rate or breathing. Scientists believe emotions originate in the brain's limbic system, which regulates emotional reactions. The limbic system comprises several structures, including the amygdala. This area plays a crucial role in processing emotions like fear and anger.

Emotions serve many functions in our lives, such as helping us interpret and respond to the world, communicate with others, and regulate our behaviour. They provide invaluable insight into our internal states and enable us to make decisions based on needs or desires. Though emotions may sometimes feel overwhelming or difficult to manage, they remain an essential element of the human experience of everyday living.

Each emotion affects our physiological state. Fear, for instance, releases adrenaline and cortisol, triggering the "fight or flight" response: increasing heart rate, causing shallow, rapid breathing, tensing up muscles. Conversely, happiness increases endorphins, which produce feelings of pleasure and reduce pain, leading to a relaxed state with slower heart rates and deeper breaths. Understanding these effects helps us better manage them and cope with them effectively.

Emotions are essential in our lives, serving a variety of functions. Not only do they bring us joy and sorrow, but they can also assist us with decision-making processes like:

Understanding our emotions: Emotions give us insight into how we feel about various situations, people, or things. They tell us if we're content, sad, scared, or excited.

Communication: Our emotions allow us to express how we feel to others. We may cry or appear distressed if we feel unhappy, so others know we need comfort. When we're happy, we smile or laugh to show everyone we're having fun.

Decision-making processes: Emotions can guide us when making choices. For instance, if something causes us fear, we might decide not to engage. If something makes us happy during an activity, we may repeat it.

Motivation: Our emotions can spur us on to take action. When we're excited or curious about something, we're more likely to explore and learn. Feeling proud of our accomplishments fuels us with energy to work harder and achieve even more successes.

Social connections: Emotions provide us with opportunities to form deep and lasting connections with those close to us. When we experience love, gratitude, or empathy, it's easier to build strong bonds with friends and family.

Survival: Fear is an emotion that helps us stay safe. When we feel threatened, our body responds in order to prepare us to escape or protect ourselves.

Learning: Emotions can teach us important lessons about life. For instance, feeling sad when a friend is injured might prompt us to be more cautious and considerate in our future actions.

Emotions are essential tools for human survival; they guide our decisions and connect us to others. Emotions are integral to who we are and play a crucial role in maintaining our mental and physical health.

3

The Vital Importance Of Emotions
HOW THEY HELP US SURVIVE AND THRIVE

Emotions play a vital role in keeping us alive and secure on a daily basis. They provide us with various benefits, such as:

Recognising danger: Fear is an essential emotion that helps us identify potential threats. When we feel threatened, our body responds by raising our heart rate and bracing us to either engage the threat or flee (the "fight or flight" response). This helps us act quickly and stay safe from harm.

Real-life examples:

1. Imagine walking alone at night. You hear footsteps coming from behind. Fear sets in, prompting you to move to a well-lit area with more people around for protection.
2. You detect gas in your home, and fear arises at the potential danger of a leak. You quickly turn off the supply and call for a professional.

Maintaining relationships: Positive emotions such as love, happiness and gratitude help us form bonds with other people. Strong social ties aid mental and physical wellbeing, offering us support, motivation and protection.

Real-life examples:

1. You enjoy spending time with friends, so you attempt to schedule regular get-togethers to strengthen your bond.
2. You express gratitude towards your parents for their support; making them feel appreciated and loved nurtures the family relationship.

Guiding our actions: Emotions such as anger or frustration can be a warning that something is amiss, motivating us to take action to rectify the situation. For instance, if we feel treated unfairly, anger could drive us to advocate for ourselves or seek justice.

Real-life examples:

1. Your colleague takes credit for your work, which makes you angry. So, to resolve the matter, you decide to speak with your manager and explain the situation in order to reach an understanding.
2. You feel frustrated with the slow progress on a group project, so you take the initiative and organise a meeting to discuss ways to enhance efficiency.

Encourage self-care: When we feel overwhelmed, exhausted or sad, our emotions can be a cue that it's time for some me time and self-care. We can regain strength and resilience by taking breaks and seeking support from others.

Real-life examples:

1. You feel exhausted after a long and stressful week at work. You take a day off to rest, recharge, and practise self-care activities.
2. You feel overwhelmed with personal problems, so call a friend or counsellor for emotional support and advice.

Learning from experiences: Feeling guilty or regret can teach us valuable lessons. If we feel guilty about a mistake, we're more likely to learn from it and prevent repeating the same error.

Real-life examples:

1. You forget your friend's birthday, so feel guilty. Draw on this experience and set reminders for important dates in the future.
2. You feel guilty for not studying enough for an exam and receive a low grade. Therefore, you create a study plan and dedicate more time to it.

Enhancing problem-solving: Curiosity and interest can motivate us to explore new ideas and draw from our experiences. We can better adapt to difficulties and make informed decisions by seeking knowledge, understanding, and insight.

Real-life examples:

1. Curiosity can drive you to research a topic you aren't familiar with for an academic project, giving you more insight and the chance to develop creative solutions.
2. Your desire to master a new skill propels you to enrol in a workshop or online class, honing your abilities and increasing your knowledge base.

When emotions go wrong

When emotions strike, people may experience various thoughts depending on the specific emotion felt.

Here are some examples of thoughts someone might have during different emotions:

Sadness:

- "I miss my friends so much. I don't know how I'll get through this without them."
- "Why do bad things always happen to me? I feel like I don't deserve happiness."

Extreme: People may isolate themselves from friends and family, leading to increased loneliness and a weakened support network.

Anger:

- "I can't believe they lied to me! How could they breach my trust like that?"
- "My coworker took credit for my work again! I'm so tired of being taken advantage of."

Extreme: In a moment of frustration, someone might say hurtful words to a loved one, potentially damaging their relationship or causing lasting emotional trauma.

Fear:

- *"What if I fail the test? Will I never get into a good college? Is my future destroyed?"*
- *"I'm scared to walk home alone at night - what if someone tries to hurt me?"*

Extreme: Fear can paralyse you, preventing you from taking on new challenges or opportunities and ultimately hindering your personal growth and success.

Happiness:

- *"I finally secured the job I've always wanted! I can't wait to start this new chapter of my life!"*
- *"Spending time with my family makes me so contented. Cherish these moments."*

Extreme: Feeling overwhelmed by happiness may cause overconfidence or carelessness, and lead to poor decision-making or a disregard for potential risks.

Frustration:

- *"No matter how hard I try, it seems impossible for me to lose weight. It's so frustrating!"*
- *"Why won't my computer work? I've tried everything. Nothing seems to fix the issue."*

Extreme: Frustration can lead someone to act out against others, creating conflicts in personal or professional relationships.

Anxiety:

- *"What if I make a mistake during my presentation? Everyone will think I'm stupid."*
- *"I feel overwhelmed with tasks. There's too much to do! I feel like drowning in responsibilities."*

Extreme: Suffering from anxiety can lead to a panic attack that can debilitate and hinder one's daily activities.

It's essential to remember that emotions are an inevitable part of life and can be managed effectively in healthy ways. This could involve practising self-awareness, seeking professional help or finding effective coping strategies for dealing with intense feelings.

We need to be aware of what we feel and how ignoring our emotions can lead us to harm.

4

When Emotions Take Over
EXPLORING THE CAUSES AND CONSEQUENCES OF EMOTIONAL OUTBURSTS

Someone who has suppressed their emotions for some time may experience an emotional outburst when confronted with a triggering event. The intensity of emotion can be overwhelming, leading to behaviours such as shouting, crying, throwing things, or even physical aggression.

Psychological explanations for why we may act out when our emotions get the better of us can vary. They may come from childhood experiences, trauma, or coping mechanisms. For instance, if we were raised in an environment that did not validate or acknowledge our emotions, it can be hard to manage them as adults. We may have learned how to suppress or avoid them entirely, making it difficult to recognise and manage them effectively.

Trauma can have an impact on how we manage our emotions. If we have experienced trauma in the past, it may impact how well we regulate our feelings in present-day situations. We may feel overwhelmed with certain feelings, or have trouble trusting others, making building healthy relationships difficult.

Many reasons can cause emotional outbursts, from feeling overwhelmed by an experience to not feeling heard or understood. Sometimes, individuals may struggle with controlling their feelings, leading them to use outbursts as a coping mechanism.

Coping mechanisms can have a major influence on our ability to manage emotions. If we use unhealthy coping methods, such as abusing drugs or alcohol to numb ourselves emotionally, it may become harder to manage those feelings effectively. Furthermore, many of us struggle with recognising or expressing them in healthy ways.

When managing emotions, it's important to be honest with yourself. Although it can be tempting to blame others for our feelings, remember that we are the ones in control of how we react in different situations. Therefore, taking responsibility for how we handle different scenarios requires self-awareness and honesty with ourselves.

Many situations can cause emotional outbursts. Each individual experiences them differently.

Common triggers for emotional outbursts include:

Feeling overwhelmed or stressed: This could be due to work or personal issues such as financial or relationship troubles.

Feeling unheard or misunderstood: When someone feels their thoughts and feelings are not acknowledged, it can lead to frustration and even anger.

Dealing with past traumas or emotional wounds: Memories or experiences from the past may cause intense emotions, leading to an outburst.

Struggling with mental health issues: Conditions such as depression, anxiety, or bipolar disorder can make it difficult to regulate emotions and may lead to outbursts of anger or frustration.

Facing unexpected or negative changes: When someone experiences a sudden loss, life change, or bad event, they may feel overwhelmed with intense emotions and outbursts.

Substance abuse: Use of drugs or alcohol can reduce inhibitions, leading to impulsive behaviour, including emotional outbursts.

It is important to recognise that emotional outbursts show deeper-seated emotional or psychological issues, and may indicate someone needs support or help to manage their emotions healthily.

Emotions can activate the "fight or flight" response in the body. This physiological reaction prepares us to defend against perceived threats by releasing hormones like adrenaline and cortisol into the bloodstream.

For example, when someone encounters a potentially hazardous situation, such as a car accident or physical altercation, their body's "fight or flight" response is activated. The increased heart rate and respiration provide energy to fight or flee the threat, while elevated blood pressure helps deliver oxygen and nutrients to muscles.

Science has shown that emotions are more than simple reactions; our thoughts, perceptions, and experiences shape them. If someone is feeling sad during an outburst, they may cry uncontrollably and express despair or hopelessness. They may say things like *"I can't take it anymore"* or *"I feel so alone."*

Sometimes, people may choose not to express their emotions verbally during an outburst and instead express them through physical gestures, such as throwing objects or hitting walls.

It is essential to remember that during an emotional outburst, people may not think clearly or rationally, and their words or actions may not accurately reflect their true feelings or intentions. Outbursts show emotional struggles and may require support in managing those emotions healthily. When these emotions are activated, they start a complex physiological response that prepares the body to deal with perceived threats.

Also crucial to managing emotional outbursts is to be aware of the psychological causes behind why we may act out our emotions in certain ways. By understanding these triggers, we can take steps to manage them better and enhance our overall well-being. This could include seeking professional help from a therapist, practising mindfulness techniques, or developing healthy coping mechanisms.

What you can start doing today:

- Find a quiet spot: Select an area where you won't be disturbed, such as a park or room in your house.
- Take deep breaths: Inhale through your nose, hold for several seconds, and then exhale through your mouth.
- Observe your thoughts: Try to observe your thoughts and emotions without judgement and bring the focus back to your breath when the mind wanders.

Reflect on past emotional reactions:

Identify the situation: Reflect on a situation in which you experienced emotional reactions and write down all relevant details, such as who was involved, where it occurred, and what caused your response.

Analyse your reaction: Reflect on how you responded to that situation and write down any thoughts or feelings that came to mind. This is where you need to be honest with yourself.

Identify what you could have done differently:

Consider how you could have handled the situation differently, then write down some strategies you can use in the future to manage your emotions more effectively.

Journal your emotions:

Commit to writing in a journal daily or every other day.

Some ideas for you:

- How am I feeling today?
- What emotions did I experience throughout the day?
- What events or situations triggered these emotions?
- Did my emotions affect my behaviour or interactions with others?
- How did I respond to my emotions?
- Are there any patterns in my emotions or reactions that I notice?
- What can I learn from my emotions today?
- Did I practise any coping skills or strategies to manage my emotions today?
- What can I do differently tomorrow to better manage my emotions?
- What am I grateful for today?

Emotional outbursts can have severe repercussions, such as harm to personal relationships, physical harm, or legal proceedings. With proper management and self-awareness, it is possible to learn how to express emotions constructively and healthily.

5

Debunking Common Misconceptions
UNRAVELLING THE MYTHS AROUND EMOTIONS

There are many common misconceptions surrounding emotions. Here are just a few and what you can do about them:

Myth: Emotions are a sign of weakness.

Emotions are an inherent part of being human and do not indicate weakness. By accepting and understanding our emotions, we can grow personally and cultivate healthier relationships with those around us.

What you can do:

Practise self-compassion: Remind yourself that it's okay to feel emotions and that they are part of life. When experiencing strong emotions, aim to avoid self-judgement or criticism.

Share your emotions with others: Be vulnerable and share your emotions with trusted friends or family members. Doing this can build stronger connections, reduce the stigma around vulnerability, and remind yourself that everyone experiences emotions; it's an inevitable part of life.

Myth: Negative emotions are always bad.

Negative emotions serve a purpose by alerting us to potential issues or teaching us valuable lessons. It is essential to acknowledge and learn from these feelings.

What you can do:

Maintain a feelings journal: Keep track of your negative emotions as they arise, along with the circumstance that caused them. Doing this helps you identify patterns and understand what triggers these feelings, enabling you to address any underlying issues and draw from your experiences.

Practise mindfulness meditation: When negative emotions come up, take a moment to observe and acknowledge them. Mindfulness meditation helps you develop an accepting awareness of your emotions without judgement, making it easier to accept them and learn from them rather than allowing them to control your decisions or thoughts.

Myth: People can completely control their emotions.

While we can learn to manage our feelings, expecting total control is unrealistic. Instead, focus on understanding yourself and developing healthy coping mechanisms.

What you can do:

Emotion regulation techniques: Adopt emotion regulation techniques such as deep breathing exercises or progressive muscle relaxation to help you better manage your emotions. Doing so can give you a sense of balance and control during stressful moments.

Set realistic expectations: Accept that emotions are natural and that it's impossible to always feel happy or calm. Adjust your expectations accordingly, striving for emotional flexibility instead of total control; this will enable you to navigate life's difficulties with resilience and adaptability.

Myth: People are emotionally dead.

Everyone experiences emotions, but some may express or process them differently. We must respect individual differences and not judge others based on emotional expression.

What you can do:

Active listening: When engaging with someone who may not express their emotions outwardly, focus on paying close attention to their words and body language. Ask open-ended questions to prompt them to share their feelings, showing empathy and respect for the unique way each individual expresses emotion.

Foster an inclusive environment: Create a safe and supportive space for people of all emotional expressions to feel safe sharing their feelings. Encourage open communication, while respecting everyone's unique ways of processing and expressing emotions - whether verbally or nonverbally.

Myth: Crying is indicative of weakness or instability.

Crying is an entirely natural expression of emotions and can be a healthy way to release stress or sadness without signifying vulnerability or instability. It does not indicate any inherent incapacity whatsoever.

What you can do:

Normalise crying: Encourage open discussions about the importance and advantages of crying. Share your own experiences of grieving and its cathartic effects, helping others see that it's a healthy way to express emotions.

Support others by offering empathy and comforting presence: When you see someone crying, offer them your listening ear or comforting presence.

You can help create an accepting atmosphere by being empathetic and supportive, where people feel free to express their emotions without fear of judgement or criticism.

Myth: Men should not express their emotions.

Emotional expression is essential for everyone, regardless of gender. Promoting open communication about feelings can improve mental health and overall well-being.

What you can do:

Encourage emotional education: Advocate for emotional literacy programs in schools and community settings that target both boys and girls alike. By instilling the importance of understanding and expressing one's emotions from an early age, society can break down gender stereotypes and create a more emotionally supportive culture.

Be a positive role model: Men, express your emotions openly and discuss them with friends, family, and peers. By setting an example of healthy emotional expression, you can help challenge traditional gender norms and foster an environment where men feel comfortable expressing their emotions without fear of judgement or rejection.

Myth: Suppressing emotions is the best way to manage them.

Suppressing feelings can lead to increased stress and mental health issues; instead, acknowledge and address your emotions appropriately.

What you can do:

Creative outlets: Explore creative outlets to express and process your emotions, such as painting, writing, dancing, or playing a musical instrument. Doing so can help release trapped feelings and give you greater insight into yourself.

Create a support network: Enlist the help of friends or family with whom you feel comfortable discussing your emotions openly. Doing this can make it easier to express feelings instead of suppressing them, ultimately leading to improved emotional wellness.

Myth: Venting your anger is always beneficial.

While expressing anger may be helpful in certain circumstances, it's essential to do so constructively. Lashing out or becoming aggressive only damages relationships and makes matters worse.

What you can do:

Practise assertiveness: Develop the ability to express your anger and frustrations assertively, without being aggressive or disrespectful. Use "I" statements when expressing your thoughts rather than attacking the individual involved. This approach encourages healthy dialogue and problem-solving amongst both parties involved.

Time-outs: If your anger is rising, step away from the situation temporarily. Use this time to decompress and consider how best to address the issue at hand. Return to the conversation with a more constructive mindset once you've regained control over your emotions.

Myth: Emotional people are irrational.

Being emotional does not automatically make someone an irrational individual. Emotions provide valuable information that can be used alongside logic to make informed decisions.

What you can do:

Develop emotional intelligence: Develop your emotional intelligence by becoming more self-aware, learning how to manage your emotions, and developing empathy for others. You can better balance emotional and rational thought processes by comprehending how emotions influence decision-making.

Reflect on past experiences: Examine times when emotions played a role in your decision-making, and evaluate the outcomes. Doing this will help you recognise patterns and learn how to better integrate emotions and rational thoughts, leading to improved overall decision-making in the future.

Myth: You can always tell how someone feels by their facial expressions.

While facial expressions can provide cues about emotions, they are not always accurate. People may try to hide or mask their feelings and some emotions are more subtle. Communicate and ask questions to truly comprehend someone's emotional state,

What you can do:

Develop observation skills: Pay careful attention to body language, tone of voice and other nonverbal cues. By honing this ability, you can become more in tune with others' emotions, even when their facial expressions may be misleading.

Promoting open dialogue: Create an atmosphere that encourages open communication and trust, where people feel comfortable discussing their emotions. Ask open-ended questions and practice active listening to gain a better insight into someone's true feelings beyond facial expressions.

Imagine your friend seems overwhelmed but is trying to maintain a brave face. To encourage open dialogue and better understand their feelings, you could create an encouraging atmosphere by saying, *"I noticed you seem a bit down today. If you'd like to talk about it…"*

Start by asking open-ended questions like, *"What's been on your mind lately?"* or *"How have you been feeling these past few days?"*

As your friend begins to express their emotions, practise active listening by paying them your full attention, maintaining eye contact and offering verbal or non-verbal cues that you're engaged. Resist the urge to interrupt or offer solutions immediately, as this could make the person feel unheard or dismissed. Instead, focus on understanding their emotions, empathising with their experience, and offering support - even if their facial expressions may not fully convey their feelings.

This approach can give you a deeper insight into their psychological state, even when facial expressions may not fully convey how you may feel inside.

How can this help you too?

Engaging in open dialogue and active listening with others can also contribute to your emotional education about yourself in several ways:

Increased self-awareness: As you listen to others share their emotions and experiences, you may notice similarities or differences in your emotional responses. This can give you a better insight into how you feel and react in various situations.

Enhancing empathy: Actively listening to others' emotions will help you develop empathy and the capacity for understanding and sharing their feelings. Furthermore, as you become more empathetic, you'll become more aware of your emotions and how they shape how you relate to others.

Emotional vocabulary: By engaging in conversations about emotions, you'll acquire new ways to describe and express your feelings. Having a more comprehensive emotional vocabulary can help you more accurately recognise and convey your emotions - an essential aspect of emotional education.

Enhancing emotional intelligence: By having open discussions about emotions and practising active listening techniques, you'll develop essential emotional intelligence abilities that will serve you both personally and professionally.

Learning from others: Gaining new perspectives and strategies for handling your emotions by listening to others' experiences. This can expand your emotional toolbox and build resilience in the face of difficulties.

In conclusion, engaging in open dialogue and active listening not only helps you comprehend the emotions of others but also builds your emotional education, self-awareness, empathy, emotional intelligence, and overall well-being.

6

The Fascinating Science Of Emotions
FAMOUS STUDIES

There are various schools of thought on the science of emotions, offering valuable insight into this wide-ranging subject. Here are a few of the most famous ones:

Emotional Intelligence: Understanding and Managing Emotions

Salovey and Mayer introduced the concept of emotional intelligence, which involves being able to recognise, understand, and manage our own emotions, and those of others.

The study concluded that emotional intelligence plays an integral role in personal and professional success; by improving our emotional intelligence, we can improve interpersonal relationships, communication abilities, and overall well-being.

They also concluded, *"Your emotions help you make good decisions and think more creatively."* For example, being more equipped to recognise emotions and express them effectively may reduce conflicts with friends or family members.

The Broaden-and-Build Theory: The Power of Positive Emotions

Fredrickson developed the Broaden-and-Build Theory, which suggests that positive emotions broaden our cognitive and behavioural repertoires, enabling us to build personal resources and resilience.

By cultivating positive emotions like gratitude or joy, we can improve our well-being, enhance problem-solving abilities, and bolster resilience when faced with difficulties.

For instance, expressing gratitude often can make us happier and more content overall. We will also be able to endure more of life's challenges.

Universal Facial Expressions: A Biological Basis for Emotion

In this study, Ekman and Friesen examined whether certain facial expressions of emotions are universal across cultures. They discovered that some fundamental aspects of emotional expression are shared among diverse human populations, suggesting a biological basis for emotional expression.

Recognising the universality of facial expressions can improve our comprehension of emotions in different cultural contexts and increase empathy with others.

For instance, being aware of facial expressions associated with certain emotions may make us better able to comprehend and connect with people from diverse backgrounds more easily.

The Undoing Effect: How Positive Emotions Help Us Recover From Stress

In this study, Fredrickson and her colleagues explored the role of positive emotions in recovering from negative emotional effects such as stress. They discovered that positive emotions can help "undo" these effects and promote faster recovery from negative ones.

By cultivating positive emotions in our daily lives, we may improve our capacity for rebounding from stress and maintain better mental health overall.

For instance, making time for activities that bring us joy or fulfilment may better equip us to cope with life's inevitable stresses.

7

The Power Of Cognitive Behavioural Therapy

CBT (cognitive behavioural therapy) is a type of therapy that seeks to identify and alter negative thought patterns and behaviours. Studies have demonstrated its efficacy in treating various mental health conditions, such as anxiety, depression, and post-traumatic stress disorder (PTSD). You can improve your overall well-being and lead a more fulfilling life by learning to control your thoughts and emotions better.

CBT helps you identify and combat negative thought patterns and behaviours. You will work with a therapist to identify triggers and false beliefs, then develop strategies for managing feelings associated with those events. Through CBT, you can learn to recognise patterns that lead to these emotions and develop more adaptive ways of thinking and responding in the future.

Studies on the effectiveness of CBT for treating mental health issues have been published widely. For instance, one study published in The Journal of Consulting and Clinical Psychology demonstrated its success at treating depression among adolescents and adults alike, while another published in Anxiety Disorders showed promise with CBT treatments for anxiety disorders.

Coping strategies

CBT offers a range of coping strategies that can be helpful when managing emotions. Here are a few:

Challenge negative thoughts: One of the core principles of CBT is challenging negative thoughts. When you catch yourself engaging in negative self-talk, try to identify its underlying beliefs and question whether they are accurate; ask if there is evidence to back up these assertions.

Practise mindfulness: Mindfulness is the art of being present in the moment without judgement or assessment. It can be beneficial in managing emotions by providing an opportunity to observe thoughts and feelings without getting consumed by them. Try dedicating a few minutes each day to mindfulness practice.

Use positive self-talk: Positive self-talk involves replacing negative thoughts with affirmations to boost self-esteem and manage negative emotions. Try replacing negative thoughts with affirmations such as, *"I am worthy"* or *"I am capable."*

Practise relaxation techniques: Relaxation techniques such as deep breathing, progressive muscle relaxation, or visualisation can help manage emotions. These practices reduce stress and promote relaxation.

Engage in pleasant activities: Scheduling time for enjoyable activities that make you feel happy and fulfilled can be beneficial when managing emotions. Make time for things that make you smile, such as spending quality time with loved ones, following a hobby, or taking a relaxing bath.

Common cognitive distortions observed during CBT

Black and white thinking: This can lead to an extreme perspective, seeing everything as good or bad with no in-between. This kind of mindset often leads to negative self-talk and judgement from others.

What this can cause:

- **Anxiety:** People who engage in black-and-white thinking experience anxiety about making mistakes or not meeting their high standards.
- **Perfectionism:** Perfectionism can manifest when someone believes that everything must be done perfectly or else the task is unworthy of the effort.
- **Negative self-talk:** Black-and-white thinking can lead to negative self-talk, where people beat themselves up over mistakes or perceived failures.
- **Depression:** This type of thinking may contribute to feelings of worthlessness which ultimately lead to feelings of hopelessness - leading to feelings of depression.
- **Relationship issues:** Black-and-white thinking can have a detrimental effect on relationships, as people may judge others harshly for not living up to their expectations or push others away out of fear of being hurt.

Catastrophising: This occurs when you imagine the worst-case scenario occurring in a given situation. You might exaggerate minor issues or assume that one setback will lead to a series of negative outcomes.

For example:

- Somebody may fear they will fail a job interview and never get hired, leading to financial ruin and homelessness.
- After having an argument with a friend, one may assume the friendship is over and they won't speak again.
- Some may fear visiting the dentist for fear of excruciating pain and potential complications.
- A student may believe one poor grade on a test will mean failing the entire course and never graduating.
- Some passengers may experience anxiety during a plane ride, fearing any turbulence or delay will result in a fatal crash.

Mind-reading: When you make assumptions about another person's thoughts or emotions without any evidence to back them up, it can be easy to become paralysed with anxiety or insecurity.

For example:

- One may assume their partner is angry with them for not responding to a text message, leading to worry and insecure feelings.
- Someone may suspect their co-worker of gossiping behind their back, even if there is no proof to back this up. This can lead to feelings of mistrust and paranoia.
- Individuals may assume their friend is upset with them for declining an invitation to hang out, leading to feelings of rejection and sadness.
- One may assume their boss is dissatisfied with their work despite receiving no feedback to support this notion. This can lead to feelings of inadequacy and self-doubt.
- Someone may feel judged or condemned by family members due to their lifestyle choices, leading them to experience feelings of shame and guilt.

Personalisation: Assuming responsibility for things outside your control can lead to feelings of guilt or blame for others. Personalisation can manifest in many forms, such as taking responsibility for someone else's negative emotions without meaning it to be your fault or making yourself the cause of something someone else feels bad about.

For example:

- When a friend cancels on you, you might assume it's because they don't enjoy spending time with you. This can lead to feelings of rejection and self-doubt.
- Your partner seems unhappy and you assume this is due to something in your past that caused it, leading to feelings of guilt or anxiety.
- Your boss criticises your work and you immediately assume it's because of inadequacy, leading to feelings of self-doubt and inadequacy.
- Your child misbehaves in public and you assume it's a reflection on you as parents, leading to feelings of guilt or shame.
- A stranger on the street gives you a dirty look and you assume it's due to something in your clothing or how you appear, leading to feelings of self-consciousness and insecurity.

Filtering: This occurs when you focus only on the negative aspects of a situation while neglecting its positive aspects. For example, you might ignore compliments or only remember critical feedback.

For example:

Scenario: After completing a project, you receive several complimentary remarks from colleagues and clients; however, one person points out a minor oversight.

Thoughts: *"I feel like such a failure for making that mistake. I always get things wrong!"*

Emotions: Feeling disappointed, anxious and insecure about your abilities.

Scenario: You and someone special go out on a date and have an enjoyable evening, but later that night they don't respond to your text message.

Thoughts: *"They must not have had a great time. I probably said something stupid."*

Emotions: Feeling rejected, anxious and self-critical.

Scenario: You give a presentation at work and receive mostly positive feedback, but your boss points out a few areas for improvement.

Thoughts: *"I can't believe I made those errors. I'm never going to be good enough for this job."*

Emotions: Feeling discouraged, anxious and self-critical.

Overgeneralisation: When you make blanket statements about yourself, others, or situations based on one negative experience, such as assuming that failure means failure for life or rejection means unlovability, you could be making sweeping judgements about yourself, others and situations without ever really knowing the context.

For example:

- Once someone is turned down for a job, they may begin to believe that finding an enjoyable career is impossible and feel defeated.
- One student may receive one disappointing grade and then conclude they lack the intelligence to succeed in their field of study.
- Someone may have a negative interaction with someone from one group and then assume that everyone from that same group feels similarly.
- After one unsuccessful attempt at a new hobby or skill, someone may assume they are unsuited for it and give up altogether.

By becoming aware of these patterns of overthinking, you can begin to challenge them with evidence-based techniques and tools provided by CBT. Challenging negative thoughts and developing coping strategies can help you to regulate your feelings more effectively, leading to a richer life with greater fulfilment.

Now try this

Black and white thinking: Recognise when your thinking is extreme and label the thoughts as "all-or-nothing." This will help to calm the emotions.

Challenge these thoughts by asking if they are 100% accurate, and if there is any evidence to back up an opposing perspective.

Reframe your thinking by finding the middle ground between extremes and taking a more balanced perspective.

Catastrophising: Catastrophising can be a harmful habit. Recognise when you're doing this and label the thoughts as "worst-case scenario."

Ask yourself if the outcome is as dire as you believe or if there are other possible outcomes that are more probable. Say to yourself what those outcomes could be.

Mind-reading: Recognise when you are making assumptions about what others are thinking or feeling and label the thoughts as "mind-reading."

Challenge these thoughts by seeking evidence to back up your assumptions or if there are other possible explanations for the person's behaviour. Could they be having a bad day? Have they got things on their mind that may be impacting them?

Reframe your thinking by focusing on what you know and communicating directly with the other person to clarify their thoughts or feelings.

Personalisation: Recognise when you're taking responsibility for things beyond your control and label these thoughts *"personalisation."*

Challenge these thoughts by asking yourself if you are responsible for the situation or if there are other factors at play. Be honest with yourself. Even just stopping to do this will de-escalate your negative emotions.

Filtering: Recognise when you are only considering the negative aspects of a situation and label these thoughts as *"filtering."*

Challenge these beliefs by asking yourself whether there are any positive elements present or if there is a more balanced perspective available. Say to yourself what the positives are, no matter how small.

Reframe your thinking by emphasising the positive aspects of a situation and challenging negative thoughts with evidence to the contrary.

Overgeneralisation: Recognise when you're making blanket statements based on one negative experience and label these thoughts *"overgeneralisation."*

Challenge these thoughts by asking yourself if the situation is as black and white as it seems, or if there are other potential outcomes or perspectives.

Test out these thoughts by asking yourself if there is any evidence to back them up.

8

What You Can And Can't Control

Recognising our limits is essential when dealing with life. While we may not have control over someone else's behaviour or what they say to us, our response to those events can make all the difference in how empowered and less overwhelmed we feel.

Here are a few ways we can take back control of our emotions:

Focusing on what is within our power to influence helps us feel in control of our destiny more effectively. Create an intention for how you want to feel and approach the day by taking deep breaths and visualising yourself feeling calm and focused. Doing this helps you start the day with a positive outlook and prevents getting overwhelmed by external factors.

Take a few moments throughout the day to pause and focus on your breath. Try not to judge or criticise your thoughts or emotions, and bring the focus back to your breath when your mind wanders. Doing this helps you stay present in the moment as well as reduce stress and anxiety levels.

Pay attention to situations or people that cause negative emotions for you, such as traffic, challenging co-workers or family members who push buttons. Once identified, develop strategies for managing those emotions when they arise.

When faced with difficult circumstances, focus on what you can control: Your thoughts and actions. Recognise that while you cannot influence others' behaviour or external events, you do have some influence over how you respond to them.

Here are some real-life examples of things over which you have control:

Your sleep schedule: You have the freedom to choose when you go to bed and when you wake up, ensuring you get enough rest so you feel refreshed and energised in the morning.

Your morning routine: You have the power to decide whether or not you have breakfast, exercise, or meditate in the morning. By making healthy decisions in this area, you can set a positive tone for the remainder of the day.

Your attitude: You have the power to decide how you respond to challenging circumstances or negative emotions. By focusing on the positive and practising gratitude, you can foster a more upbeat outlook on life.

Your communication style: You have the power to choose how you communicate with others, whether that be through active listening, clear and respectful language, or empathetic responses.

Your personal boundaries: You have the power to set and enforce boundaries in both your personal and professional life to safeguard your time, energy, and well-being.

Start with the small things first and watch your mood change:

Some ideas for you:

- A warm cup of tea or coffee in the morning.
- A hug or kiss from a loved one.
- A beautiful sunset or sunrise.
- A good hair day.
- A favourite song on the radio.
- A delicious meal or snack.
- A cosy blanket or a comfortable bed.
- A good book or movie.
- A kind gesture from a stranger.
- A funny joke or moment that made you laugh.

Reflect on your day: Before hitting the hay, take a few moments to review your day. Consider any stressful or challenging situations and how they affected you emotionally; celebrate successes and identify areas for improvement when managing emotions.

- What was the most challenging situation I faced today?
- How did I react emotionally to that situation?
- Was my emotional response helpful or unhelpful in that situation?
- What could I have done differently to manage my emotions more effectively?
- What were some positive moments from my day that made me feel good?
- Did I take time to practise self-care today? If not, how can I incorporate self-care into my routine tomorrow?
- Did I communicate effectively with others today? If not, how can I improve my communication skills in the future?
- How did my values and beliefs influence my emotional reactions today?
- What am I grateful for today?
- What steps can I take tomorrow to continue managing my emotions effectively?

What you may have tried before and why it didn't work:

You may have tried different strategies to manage your emotions, such as ignoring or suppressing them.

Here are some common excuses people use to avoid managing their emotions:

- *"I don't have time for this right now; I'll deal with it later."*
- *"It's not a big deal, so why should I bother?"*
- *"If I ignore my emotions, they will go away."*
- *"I don't want others to deal with my problems."*
- *"I'm afraid to confront my emotions and what they might signify."*

While these strategies may provide temporary comfort, they are ineffective long-term and make managing emotions more challenging. Neglecting or suppressing feelings can lead to overwhelm, anxiety, and depression.

It is essential to remember that managing emotions is an ongoing process that necessitates self-awareness, honesty and the willingness to ask for help when needed. If these strategies haven't worked in the past, consider seeking professional assistance from a therapist or counsellor who can teach you healthy coping mechanisms and assist in better managing your feelings.

9

Understanding How Values And Beliefs Influence Your Emotional Reactions

Reflecting on your values and how they influence emotional reactions means you can work to align those emotions with your beliefs and become more authentic in your interactions with yourself and others when faced with difficult choices.

Here are some examples of values:

Compassion: Compassion can be demonstrated through acts of kindness, generosity, and empathy towards others. When times are good, someone with this value may volunteer or donate to charities to help those less fortunate. On the flip side, when negative emotions get in the way, they may still try their best to be kind but become defensive or self-centred instead.

Honesty: Honesty can be demonstrated through speaking truthfully and being authentic with oneself and others. When life is going well, someone with this value may share their successes and challenges openly with those around them. Conversely, when negative emotions get in the way, they may struggle to express themselves honestly or avoid confrontations altogether leaving a feeling of isolation or irritability.

Responsibility: Responsibility can be demonstrated through taking ownership of one's actions and decisions. When life is going well, someone with this value might make plans and stick to them, taking responsibility for any errors or setbacks. On the other hand, when emotions get in the way, they may blame others or external elements instead of taking accountability for their own role in a situation causing conflicts.

Creativity: Creativity can be seen in innovative solutions to problems and creative expression through art or other artistic outlets. When life is good, someone with this value may spend time pursuing hobbies or projects they enjoy. Unfortunately, when negative emotions get in the way, they may become stuck in negative thought patterns or feel uninspired and unmotivated.

By understanding how your values and beliefs affect and influence your emotional reactions, you can take the next step towards your own mental well-being and master the art of tolerating people with different values and beliefs which may not align with your own - and that's ok. It takes a little bit of everyone to make the world we live in the wonderful and stimulating place it is.

10

Go Back To Come Forward
COUNSELLING AND HOW IT CAN HELP YOU

Tackling our triggers and past experiences can be a difficult, yet essential part of understanding our emotions. By exploring the root causes of these reactions, we gain an understanding of our thought patterns, behaviours, and coping mechanisms.

With increased self-awareness comes a greater capacity to identify and manage triggers more efficiently - leading to reduced emotional reactions and an overall sense of control over lives.

Trauma can have a significant effect on our emotional well-being, often leading to negative emotions such as jealousy, isolation, depression and anger. These reactions stem from survival mode - our body's adaptive response to perceived threats or danger.

For instance, if we experienced trauma such as abandonment or rejection, jealousy may develop to protect ourselves from future emotional pain. Our survival mode tells us to guard our emotions and be wary of potential threats to our relationships.

Trauma can also cause us to isolate ourselves from others to protect ourselves from further harm. Our survival mode tells us it's safer to remain alone than risk being hurt again by others.

Depression is often a response to trauma, as our survival mode may cause us to shut down emotionally to conserve energy and resources. This may manifest as a lack of motivation, feelings of hopelessness, or general apathy towards life.

Finally, anger can also be a common response to trauma, as our survival mode may cause us to become defensive and lash out at perceived threats. This could be an attempt at asserting power and control in an environment where we feel vulnerable or threatened.

Overall, these emotions are connected to our survival mode and often arise as a natural reaction to trauma. However, with the right support and tools, we can learn how to better manage these feelings and move towards healing and recovery.

Seeking support from a counsellor or therapist may be beneficial in this process as they offer a safe space without judgement when discussing these matters. Therapy also provides opportunities to develop new coping skills while building emotional resilience - ultimately improving overall well-being.

Why counselling could help you

Counselling can be a great asset when it comes to managing your emotions. Counselling provides a safe and supportive space for exploring difficult feelings, with trained therapists available for guidance, support, and tools to help you tackle these difficulties head-on.

Counselling can help you recognise and manage your triggers, create effective coping strategies, and gain a more insightful understanding of yourself and your emotions. With greater self-awareness comes improved emotional regulation, strengthened relationships, as well as an overall improved sense of well-being for you.

Today, take the first step toward exploring counselling as a way to manage your emotions. Start by researching local counsellors or therapy options in your area. Ask friends or family members for recommendations if they have had success with therapy before. Once you've identified a therapist or program that speaks to you, reach out and arrange an initial appointment or consultation.

At your initial appointment with a therapist, they will likely ask you questions about your emotional challenges and goals for therapy. It also provides an opportunity for any queries regarding the counselling process and whether the therapist is suitable for you.

Counselling can be a beneficial tool to help manage your emotions and enhance your quality of life. With counselling, you'll acquire the skillset and understanding needed to navigate emotional difficulties with grace and success in both personal and professional environments.

11

Love And The Rollercoaster Of Emotions
NAVIGATING THE IMPACT OF EMOTIONAL EXPERIENCE ON YOUR RELATIONSHIP WITH YOUR PARTNER

Relationships can bring us immense joy and fulfilment, but they also present stress and emotional triggers.

This chapter is designed to help you navigate the complex emotions associated with romantic relationships, develop skills for managing conflict and deepen a connection. It will address common emotional triggers that may arise in relationships and provide strategies for recognising and managing them. We'll also cover communication techniques for handling conflicts and building stronger connections with your significant other.

It is essential to remember that relationships involve two people, but each individual plays an integral part. I urge you to be self-aware and honest about your own actions and emotions, taking responsibility for what you can control.

We will also discuss why and how relationship issues can impact us, as well as examine some tried-and-true strategies that may not have worked in the past.

By the end of this chapter, you will have all the tools necessary to foster a stronger, more rewarding connection with your significant other and have a clear and practical strategy for managing your relationship, with concrete examples and real-world applications.

How our past impacts our relationships

Our past experiences and relationships can have a significant effect on how we experience current ones emotionally.

If we experienced trauma or abandonment as children, it may be difficult for us to trust someone or fear being left again. Furthermore, patterns of behaviour developed as coping mechanisms from these experiences may still exist which negatively influence present relationships.

Being mindful of our past experiences and how they may impact our current relationships is essential. This could include watching out for unhealthy or restricting patterns of behaviour or thought. For instance, if you find yourself constantly seeking validation from your partner, this could be indicative of unresolved issues from your past.

Therapists may use techniques like cognitive-behavioural therapy or EMDR (Eye Movement Desensitisation and Reprocessing) to help clients reprocess events from the past and learn new ways of managing emotions.

The science behind this is our brain's neuroplasticity, which allows it to adapt and change depending on our experiences and behaviours. Traumatic events can have a lasting effect on our minds and emotions, but therapy and other interventions can help rewire the brain and create new neural pathways.

Overall, it's essential to recognise the impact our past experiences and relationships can have on our present emotional state and interpersonal dynamics. By acknowledging and addressing these issues, we can work toward cultivating healthier and more fulfilling connections.

Emotional triggers in romantic relationships

Emotional triggers in romantic relationships refer to situations or actions which cause strong emotions in one or both partners. Reactions may range from past experiences to current circumstances, depending on who you ask.

Some real-life examples are:

Feeling ignored or discounted: If your partner consistently fails to listen or interrupts when speaking, you may feel frustrated, hurt, and unimportant. You might ask yourself, *"Why won't they just pay attention to me? Don't they care what I have to say?"*

It may lead to a breakdown in communication and a lack of intimacy in the relationship if not addressed.

Feeling disrespected by your partner: If your partner ignores requests or boundaries, such as showing up without permission or constantly checking in on you, it can leave you feeling disrespected and violated. You might ask yourself, *"Why they can't just respect my boundaries? Don't they understand how essential this is to me?"*

This can create a lack of trust and an erosion of the emotional safety in the relationship.

Feeling jealousy or insecurity: If your partner is spending too much time with someone else or not giving you enough attention, you may feel jealous or insecure. You may ask yourself, *"Why are they spending so much time with them? Do they like them more than me? Am I not doing enough for them?"*

This can lead to controlling behaviours and a lack of independence in the relationship.

Feeling like your partner isn't showing you enough love and attention: If your partner isn't showing you enough affection or attention, you may feel neglected and unloved. You might ask yourself, *"Why won't they show me more affection? Don't they love me any longer?"*

This can lead to resentment and distance between partners.

Feeling criticised or attacked: If your partner is constantly criticising or attacking you, it can leave you feeling hurt, defensive and attacked. You may ask yourself, *"Why do they keep criticising me? Can't they see that their words hurt me?"*

This can lead to a cycle of negativity and erode trust and intimacy in the relationship.

Emotional triggers can have a powerful effect on both partners. For the person experiencing them, intense feelings such as anger, sadness or anxiety may arise. These emotions often lead to reactive behaviour which only serves to escalate conflict and further strain within the relationship.

For the other partner, it can be difficult to comprehend or respond to their partner's strong emotional reactions, leading to feelings of confusion, frustration or helplessness. If these triggers are not addressed or managed effectively, they could erode the foundation of the relationship and result in a breakdown in communication and connection between partners.

What you can start doing today

Feeling ignored or neglected:

Take a moment to calm down and consider why you're upset. Could it be that your partner didn't understand the significance of what you were saying? Once you have gained some perspective, express your feelings in an assertive, calm way using "I" statements without blaming your partner for what has gone wrong.

Try this:

Examples of "I" statements to express feeling ignored or neglected in a relationship:

- *"Interrupting me while I'm speaking causes me to feel unimportant and like my words don't matter to you."*
- *"Planning without consulting me first makes me feel left out; like you don't value my opinion."*
- *"When we don't spend enough quality time together, I feel neglected. I miss you and want to ensure that we prioritise our relationship."*

When using "I" statements, you should express your own emotions and experiences.

Additionally, consider other possible causes for their behaviour - like maybe they've been under a lot of stress at work, which might explain why they seem more absent-minded or distracted than usual. By approaching this situation with empathy and understanding, you can work together towards finding an agreeable solution that benefits everyone involved.

Feeling like your partner doesn't respect your boundaries:

It is essential to communicate your boundaries clearly and assertively with your partner. If you feel disrespected, take a step back and assess if you have been clear about what needs to be communicated. Once identified, communicate those boundaries to them calmly but respectfully.

Try this:

- *"I feel uncomfortable when you arrive unexpectedly. Can we discuss a better way of communicating when visiting?"*
- *"I need some alone time after work to decompress. Can we schedule some time when we can catch up?"*
- *"I don't appreciate it when you search my phone without my consent. Can we have a conversation about respecting each other's privacy?"*

Looking for evidence why they may be overstepping may help clarify their reasons for their actions. For instance, if they are constantly checking your phone, this could indicate insecurity or mistrust rather than an intentional disrespect of boundaries.

Feeling jealousy or insecure?:

Recognise that your feelings of jealousy or insecurity are personal and not necessarily indicative of your partner's actions. Take ownership of your emotions by communicating your worries to your significant other calmly and respectfully, acknowledging that they may not have intended for you to experience such distress.

Try this:

- *"I feel insecure when you spend time with your friends without me, and while it is not necessarily your intention to make me feel this way, how can we talk about ways to spend more quality time together?"*

- *"I understand that jealousy is not my fault, but it still worries me when I see you talking to someone else at the party. Can we try checking in more often when we're together socially?"*
- *"I'm feeling jealous right now, but it isn't because I don't trust you. I just need some assurance that our relationship matters to you. Can we arrange a date night soon?"*

Evidence may involve challenging your own assumptions and considering alternative viewpoints.

For instance, instead of assuming your partner is intentionally trying to make you jealous, consider whether there could be other explanations for their behaviour.

Feeling like you're not receiving enough love and attention:

Instead of becoming angry or resentful, communicate your needs to your partner clearly and assertively. Request specific behaviours that would make you feel more loved and appreciated while being willing to compromise and negotiate.

Try this:

- *"I feel hurt when you don't show me affection or attention, as it makes me feel unimportant and neglected."*
- *"I understand that you may be busy, but when you cancel our plans at the last minute, it leaves me disappointed and unloved."*
- *"I appreciate it when you show me affection with small gestures like hugs or kind words; it makes me feel loved and appreciated."*

Evidence to consider in this situation could include noting if your partner is going through a particularly busy or stressful period and expressing empathy and understanding while still communicating your needs.

It's essential to communicate assertively without blaming them and be willing to listen and compromise as we move forward.

Feeling critiqued:

Remain calm and listen to your partner's concerns without becoming defensive or attacking back. Validate their feelings, and seek to understand where they're coming from while also respectfully expressing your own sentiments.

Try this:

- *"When you criticise me, it leaves me feeling inadequate and unworthy. Can we discuss this more constructively?"*
- *"I appreciate your concerns about my handling of that situation, but I need to hear it in a way that doesn't feel like an attack on my character."*
- *"I appreciate that you want to help me improve, but it can be challenging for me to accept criticism without feeling defensive. Can we work on finding a way of providing feedback that feels more encouraging?"*

When seeking evidence, it can be useful to determine whether your partner's criticism comes from a place of genuine concern or care or is intended to be hurtful or demeaning.

Pay attention to any patterns in communication and whether there are underlying issues that need to be addressed within the relationship.

Common emotions in relationships

Here is a list of common emotions in relationships that may arise in a relationship, strategies for handling them, and steps to bring partners closer together:

Love: Feeling deep affection and connection to our partner can be one of the most fulfilling aspects of a relationship. Strategies for cultivating this emotion could include spending quality time together, expressing appreciation and gratitude towards one another, (what they do well, no matter how small) and engaging in shared activities or interests. Other ways to bring partners closer together might include expressing your love verbally or through gestures: prioritising your partner's needs and wants, as well as being open about your thoughts and feelings.

Fear: Fear can manifest in a relationship when we feel uncertain or insecure about its future. Strategies for dealing with this emotion could include having open and honest communication about fears or worries: setting clear boundaries and expectations, as well as seeking support or guidance from a therapist or counsellor. Steps that partners could take to bring them closer together include working through fears together: engaging in activities or experiences that build trust, and prioritising the relationship over individual fears or insecurities.

Anger: Anger can arise in a relationship when we perceive an imminent danger to our emotional or physical safety. Strategies for managing anger include taking time to cool off and reflect on the source of the emotion; expressing feelings calmly and assertively, using "I" statements instead of blame or accusations; practising forgiveness and empathy; finding common ground and working towards compromise, as well as seeking professional assistance if needed.

Jealousy: Jealousy can occur when we feel threatened or insecure about our partner's attention or affection. Strategies for managing jealousy could include acknowledging its source and addressing any underlying insecurities: building trust and open communication, as well as avoiding actions that might be seen as controlling or possessive. Steps to bring partners closer together could include practising open communication and transparency: finding ways to build trust in the relationship, as well as actively appreciating and valuing each other's qualities.

Disappointment: Disappointment can occur in a relationship when expectations are not met or there is perceived failure on our partner's part. Strategies for managing disappointment could include acknowledging and expressing feelings constructively: working together towards solutions or compromises, and focusing on positive aspects of the relationship. Steps that could bring partners closer include, finding ways to rekindle excitement and passion: practising gratitude towards one another, and actively working towards common goals or aspirations.

Quick questions

Q: How can I manage my jealousy in a relationship?

Answer: Recognise the sources of your envy and discuss them with your partner. Additionally, practise self-care techniques like exercising or meditation to help manage emotions.

Q: What can I do when my emotions in a relationship become overwhelming?

Answer: Take a step back and use self-soothing techniques such as deep breathing or journalling. Additionally, consider seeking professional assistance, such as therapy to develop coping skills and manage intense emotions.

Q: How can I effectively express my feelings in a relationship?

Answer: Use "I" statements to express how you feel and avoid blame or accusations. Listen attentively to your partner's response and work together towards finding solutions to any problems.

Q: How can I manage conflicts with my partner in a healthy way?

Answer: Practise active listening and avoid becoming defensive or attacking. Make "I" statements instead of using blame language. Work together towards finding a resolution that benefits both of you.

Q: How can I strengthen my emotional connection with my partner?

Answer: Foster vulnerability and open communication. Share your thoughts and emotions with them while actively listening to what they have to say. Plan fun activities together that will create lasting memories and deepen your bond.

12

Parental Bonds And Emotional Dynamics
EXPLORING THE IMPACT OF EMOTIONS ON YOUR RELATIONSHIP WITH YOUR PARENTS

Our relationship with our parents is one of the most essential and meaningful ones in our lives, but it can also be complex and challenging. Childhood experiences and past wounds shape how we relate to them as adults, and these dynamics have a significant effect on how emotionally healthy and secure we feel.

This chapter will address the common difficulties experienced in parent-child relationships and how to resolve them healthily. We'll also look at understanding and healing childhood wounds, as well as strategies for cultivating an encouraging and productive relationship with your parents.

By understanding how your experiences may impact your current relationship with your parents, you can take steps towards healing and improving it. This chapter offers practical advice and real-world examples to equip you with the tools and techniques needed to create a more rewarding and satisfying connection with them.

Relationships often face communication breakdowns, disagreements over boundaries, unresolved childhood wounds, and differences in values and beliefs. Here's what you can do about them:

Communication breakdowns: To handle communication breakdowns effectively, practise active listening by giving your full attention when your parent speaks and acknowledging their feelings. Clear up any misunderstandings and express yourself honestly and respectfully. Use effective communication techniques, such as using "I" statements instead of blame or criticism, to avoid unnecessary arguments or disagreements.

Try this:

If you feel your parent isn't listening to you, try using "I" statements instead of accusing or criticising them.

For instance, instead of saying, *"You never listen to me,"* try saying something like, *"I feel like my opinions aren't being heard when I talk to you."*

Doing this may help them comprehend how their actions impact you and promote more open communication in the future.

If you and your parents have different communication styles, try to find a compromise that benefits both of you.

For instance, if your dad is more direct and assertive while you prefer indirect approaches, communicate in ways that satisfy both of you - this could include asking them to use a gentler tone or explaining your thoughts more fully.

If communication has broken down because of a past argument or conflict, consider seeking the help of a mediator or therapist. A third-party neutral facilitator can help with communication and offer tools to resolve conflicts amicably.

Disagreements over boundaries: To resolve disagreements

over boundaries, have an honest and open conversation about your needs and expectations. State your boundaries clearly and respectfully, while being willing to negotiate and compromise. Respect your parent's boundaries as well, trying to find a middle ground that benefits both parties.

Try this:

Here are some real examples of what to say when disagreeing over boundaries with your parents:

- *"I appreciate your desire to help, but I need some space to figure things out on my own. Can we agree to check in with each other once a week instead of daily calls?"*
- *"I understand your concern, but we need to set some boundaries when discussing certain topics. Can we agree to focus on more positive or neutral subjects during our conversations?"*
- *"I understand your desire for what's best for me, but I need to make my own decisions and learn from my errors. Can we agree to respect each other's choices even when we don't always agree?"*

Unresolved childhood wounds: To address unresolved childhood wounds, seek professional help such as therapy or counselling. This can help you process and heal from past traumas and gain a better understanding of how they may be affecting your current relationships. Lastly, practise self-compassion and forgiveness towards yourself and your parents to foster growth and healing in both of you.

Try this:

Try asking your parents about their childhoods and experiences, and you may gain a better insight into their behaviour and attitudes toward you.

This will help foster empathy and compassion.

You could ask:

- *"Could you share with me some of your favourite memories from childhood?"*
- *"How did your parents handle conflicts or difficult situations when you were growing up?"*
- *"What was one of the biggest challenges you faced during that time, and how did you overcome it?"*

Practise self-reflection and mindfulness: Take time to examine your own triggers and patterns of behaviour, which may be connected to childhood wounds. By staying present in the moment, you can become more aware of your emotions and reactions and develop healthier ways of responding to them.

Try this:

Keep a journal to document your emotions and reactions, as well as any patterns or triggers related to childhood wounds.

Consider seeking guidance from a therapist or counsellor to develop healthy coping mechanisms and strategies for managing difficult emotions.

Use self-care activities that promote mindfulness, such as yoga, nature walks or creative hobbies.

Diversity of values and beliefs: When dealing with differences in values and beliefs with your parents, approach the conversation with an open mind and an eagerness to listen and comprehend. Respect each other's opinions and seek common ground where possible. Agree to disagree and focus on maintaining a healthy and respectful relationship despite your differences.

Try this:

To better comprehend your values and beliefs, reflect on experiences that have shaped you. Active listening when parents express their beliefs can help you gain insight into their perspective without judgement.

Here are some examples of what to say when responding:

To yourself:

- *"What are my values and beliefs, and where do they originate?"*
- *"How can I approach this conversation with an open mind and respect for my parents' views?"*
- *"How can we find common ground and maintain a healthy relationship despite our differences?"*

To your parents:

- *"I appreciate your perspective and want to understand it better."*
- *"We may not agree, but I respect your beliefs and values."*
- *"Let's focus on maintaining a healthy relationship despite our differences."*

The science behind this is that by approaching differences in values and beliefs with an open mind and willingness to listen, you can reduce conflict and build a stronger bond with your parents.

Active listening also helps you better comprehend your own views and values and foster empathy for others.

Our relationship with our parents can be complex and trying. Childhood experiences shape how we relate to them as adults, and these dynamics have an immense effect on how emotionally healthy and secure we feel.

By understanding how past hurts may impact our current relationship with our parents, we can take steps towards healing and improving it.

Start today off on a positive note by:

Practise active listening with your parent by paying full attention when they speak and acknowledging their feelings.

Avoid unnecessary arguments or disagreements by using *"I"* statements instead of blame or criticism; for instance, instead of saying, *"You never listen to me,"* try saying something like, *"I feel like my opinions aren't being heard when I talk to you."*

Remember, you are only in control of what *you* think and do.

13

Companionship And Emotional Connections

UNDERSTANDING THE ROLE OF EMOTIONS IN YOUR RELATIONSHIPS WITH FRIENDS

We all understand the importance of having healthy friendships for our mental well-being and contentment. Yet maintaining these bonds can prove challenging, particularly when facing conflicts or disagreements.

In this chapter, we'll tackle some common challenges faced by friendships and provide practical tips and strategies for creating and maintaining strong connections. We will examine the significance of taking responsibility for our actions and understanding how our behaviour impacts our friendships.

We'll also address how to communicate effectively, resolve conflicts healthily and respectfully, and explore how friendships affect our mental health and well-being, emphasising the importance of cultivating healthy connections with those around us.

It's easy to get stuck in negative patterns in our friendships and try the same unsuccessful strategies to resolve problems. This chapter offers a fresh perspective and practical tools for creating more fulfilling and positive connections with those you care about most.

Prepare to learn, develop, and strengthen your bonds with those around you!

The importance of positive friendships

Positive friendships are essential for our mental well-being and emotional health. Having people to share experiences with can increase feelings of happiness, self-worth, and belongingness while decreasing loneliness or isolation.

Friends offer comfort during times of hardship, offer us different perspectives and insights, and even help us discover new interests or hobbies. Research has proved the power of having a social support system can have many advantages for our mental and physical well-being, such as reduced stress levels, improved immune system functioning, and even an extended lifespan.

Deep friendships can enhance our communication skills, empathy and capacity to form meaningful connections with others - which has a beneficial effect on all aspects of life. Hence, cultivating healthy and fulfilling friendships should be an integral part of living a happy, healthy and rewarding life.

What about when it goes wrong?
Feeling insecure in friendships is an all too common experience that can have a significant effect on our daily lives.

This feeling may arise because of past experiences, low self-esteem, or fear of rejection. Insecurities can lead to a range of emotions, such as anxiety, jealousy and self-doubt; these negative emotions can impact how we interact with friends and our overall mental well-being.

Here are some examples of how insecurity in our friendships can manifest:

Constantly seeking validation: We may feel the urge to check in constantly with our friends to confirm they still like or value our friendship. This could involve asking for confirmation or seeking approval for what we do or say.

Always seeking validation from friends can indicate insecurity and low self-esteem. It may make you feel anxious, uncertain of yourself, and like you don't measure up to those close to you. This behaviour may manifest into over-dependence on them for emotional support, like walking on eggshells, afraid to say or do anything that might damage the friendship. This could lead to behaviours such as often apologising or avoiding conflict altogether.

Addressing this is essential for increasing your self-esteem and confidence. Engage in self-care activities that make you feel good about yourself, such as exercising, meditation or engaging in an enjoyable hobby. Reminding yourself of your positive qualities and accomplishments can be very helpful. Actively strive to replace negative self-talk with positive affirmations and build trusting relationships with your friends. Be assertive yet willing to listen and compromise when necessary.

Try this:

If you constantly seek affirmation from friends, try challenging your negative thoughts and beliefs with evidence. Assess if there is actual proof that they *"don't like you"*, or value your friendship, as you fear. Focus on objective facts rather than subjective interpretations.

Some CBT techniques you could use to address the need for validation in your friendships:

"I don't need constant validation from my friends to feel worthy and valuable."

"It's okay if they don't always agree with me or approve of everything I say or do."

"I can make my own decisions without needing their approval for everything."

"I am confident in myself and my abilities, even if my friends don't always acknowledge or validate them."

"My self-worth doesn't depend on what people think of me or our friendship."

The statements above can help you challenge and reframe negative thought patterns that may contribute to your need for constant validation from friends.

Remember:

- By practising these thoughts and beliefs regularly, you'll build up trust in yourself and feel more secure within your friendships.
- By reframing your thoughts, you can take control of your emotional state and stop seeking constant approval from others.
- By actively seeking evidence and challenging negative thoughts, you can learn to shift your focus away from needing validation from others and towards building self-confidence and self-worth.

Over-analysing actions or words: When we feel insecure, it's easy to read too much into our friend's actions or words. For instance, we may assume that a friend is upset with us because they didn't respond immediately to a text or that they don't like us as much because they cancelled plans. This type of thinking can lead to misinterpretation of their intentions and create unnecessary tension between you.

What else could it be?

One way to use CBT to combat over-analysing actions or words in friendships is by asking yourself, *"What else could it be?"*

Instead of automatically assuming negative intentions from your friend's behaviour, consider other potential explanations.

Your friend may not have responded right away because of being busy or having their phone off; they could have cancelled plans because of a family emergency or personal issue rather than disliking you.

Think of the times you may not have automatically responded to a text from a good friend.

Did you mean anything by it? Or were you busy or had something on your mind?

You can avoid jumping to conclusions and maintain a more balanced perspective by considering alternative explanations.

Feeling unworthy: Insecurity can sometimes lead us to believe that our friends don't value us or don't really want us around. We may downplay our accomplishments or feel the need to prove ourselves constantly to them.

Feeling unworthy in friendships may stem from experiences as a child, such as not feeling validated or supported by parents or peers. This may manifest in negative behaviours like always needing affirmation, being overly self-critical, or isolating ourselves from our circle of friends.

When feeling low about ourselves emotionally, we may say things like, *"I'm not good enough,"* or *"They don't really like me."*

To combat these thoughts, it is essential to recognise and challenge them; also build self-confidence and practise self-compassion to combat feelings of unworthiness.

Here are three things you can start doing today to enhance your emotional state in friendships:

Practise gratitude: Take time each day to reflect on the good aspects of your friendships and express gratitude for them. Doing this can help shift your focus from insecurity and negative thoughts to appreciation and positivity.

Ask yourself:

"What positive qualities do my friends possess that I am grateful for?"

"How have my friends positively impacted my life and well-being?"

"What are some fun and happy memories I've shared with my friends?"

"What are some ways I can show appreciation for my friends?"

"How can I focus on the good in my friendships instead of dwelling on negative thoughts or insecurity?"

Engage in self-care: Make time for activities that bring you joy and comfort, such as exercise, meditation, or hobbies. By looking after yourself, you'll be better able to manage your friendship's difficulties and maintain a positive emotional state.

Building your self-esteem: Strive to build your confidence and self-worth outside of friendships.

This could include setting personal goals and working towards them, engaging in positive self-talk, and surrounding yourself with supportive people who uplift and motivate you.

By appreciating yourself for who you are, you'll be less likely to seek validation from others and more likely to cultivate healthier, lasting relationships.

Try this:

Establish realistically achievable personal goals: Consider what you want to accomplish both short and long-term, then break those objectives into smaller, more achievable steps. Celebrate each small victory to increase your self-assurance and motivation levels.

Practise positive self-talk: Replace negative self-talk with encouraging affirmations. Focus on your strengths and accomplishments, reminding yourself of the progress you've made. Avoid comparing yourself to others; instead, focus on improving yourself for future success.

Surround yourself with supportive people. Seek those who encourage and motivate you, such as family, friends, mentors, or a support group. Take part in activities and communities that reflect your values and interests so that you can connect with like-minded individuals.

Negative people can impact us negatively because their pessimistic and critical attitudes deflate our moods and self-esteem.

When we spend time around people who consistently complain or focus on the negative, we may adopt those same attitudes and beliefs, leading to feelings of hopelessness or anxiety.

Being around supportive and positive people can boost our self-esteem, improve our outlook on life, and provide us with the encouragement we need to pursue our goals and dreams.

These individuals can offer a listening ear, helpful advice, and a sense of belonging, making us feel more motivated, confident, and fulfilled in our relationships and in life.

Seek out the supporters!

Maintaining healthy friendships can be a challenge when life gets hectic, or emotions run high. But there are steps you can take to keep your connections vibrant and healthy:

Manage your emotions: Before reaching out to friends, take a moment to manage your feelings. Try self-care activities like exercise, meditation, or deep breathing to reduce stress and calm the mind. Doing this will enable you to approach the conversation with clarity and serenity.

Check-in frequently: Make time to reach out to friends and ask open-ended questions that show you are interested in their well-being. Try not to just talk about yourself and your own problems; rather, actively listen to what they have to say and show empathy.

Try this:

"Hey! It's been a while since we spoke. How are things going for you?"

"I noticed you seemed a bit down last time we spoke. How have you been feeling lately?"

"What's been on your mind lately? If you want to discuss it, I'm more than happy to listen."

"Life can be stressful at times. What has been going on in your life recently that is causing you stress?"

"How have you been managing everything that has come your way recently?"

What if it's you who is feeling stressed or emotional?

If you're feeling stressed or overwhelmed while speaking with a friend, take a deep breath and try your best to remain present in the moment.
Remind yourself that your presence is meant to support your friend; put aside any personal feelings for now. If it helps, let your friend know if you need to take a break so that both of you can gather your thoughts and emotions.
You could say something like, *"I want to do my best for you, but I need some space to process my feelings before we continue. Can we take a brief break and resume this conversation in a few minutes?"*

By acknowledging your own emotions, as well as showing your friend that you are invested in being their support system, you both win, and the situation doesn't escalate.

Listen actively: When friends open up to you, listen intently by paying attention and validating their experiences. Avoid interrupting or offering unsolicited advice, as this may make them feel unheard or dismissed.

Try this:

If you feel your friend is not listening to you, it's essential to express your concerns in a calm and respectful way.

Try saying something like, *"I appreciate the time you took to listen, but I don't feel heard right now. Could we take a moment to regroup and make sure we're both on the same page?"* This gives both of you an opportunity to work towards improving communication.

Additionally, try practising active listening to yourself so that the behaviour you desire for your friend mirrors what you wish them to model.

Utilise technology mindfully: Texting and messaging can be convenient, but it's essential to use them mindfully. Avoid sending too many messages or expecting an instant reply. Respect your friend's boundaries and their response timeframe when sending a message.

Offer support: If your friend is going through a challenging time, show your empathy by sending them a thoughtful message, cooking dinner or making them coffee, or offering to assist them with whatever task they're facing.

Try this:

If you're feeling overwhelmed and in need of support, it is essential to express your needs to a friend politely and honestly.

For example, saying something like, *"I've been having some difficulties lately and could use some advice. Would you have some free time soon for talking or hanging out?"* When you express your needs without making demands, both of you gain an opportunity for mutual understanding and care.

Remember: it's okay to ask for help when needed; true friendships require mutual help and consideration.

Be honest: If you're feeling emotionally or spiritually overwhelmed, be honest with your friends about how you're feeling. Explain that while you may not be available as often, but still value their friendship. Doing this can prevent misunderstandings and strengthen the bond over time.

Try this:

Here are some examples of what to say to stay in control of your emotions when being honest with friends:

"Hey, just wanted to let you know that I've been feeling particularly overwhelmed lately and may not be as accessible as usual. However, our friendship remains important to me and I do hope we can still stay in touch."

"I wanted to reach out and let you know that I am facing a difficult time and could use some space or support. Thank you so much for being there for me."

"I wanted to be honest and let you know that I'm feeling emotionally spent lately. This isn't about you or our friendship, but it may be that I need to take some time for self-care."

"I value our friendship and want to be open with you about how I'm feeling. Recently, I've been facing some personal struggles that could use some extra support or understanding from you."

Maintaining healthy friendships requires effort, communication, and mutual respect.

By staying in touch, offering support, and being honest with one another, you can build on your connections while remaining resilient during any challenges that life throws your way.

14

How Emotions Impact Your Relationship With Your Boss And The Workplace Environment

No matter your level of experience or career progression, managing your relationship with your boss can be a testy and sometimes stressful endeavour. While a positive working environment and growth prospects arise from such relationships, an unhealthy one may cause feelings of frustration, disillusionment or even burnout.

In this chapter, we'll address common problems that occur in relationships with bosses, such as power dynamics and conflicts, and offer practical strategies for creating a productive working relationship. We'll also cover communication techniques that can help you manage challenging conversations with your supervisor and enhance the quality of your overall workplace experience.

It's essential to remember that while you may not have control over every aspect of your relationship with your boss, you do have some influence over yourself and how you act and react. By being self-aware and honest about how your actions impact the dynamic, you can take steps to improve it and foster a more supportive work environment for yourself.

Through this chapter, you will see concrete examples and real-world applications to help you implement these strategies in your workplace, and introduce you to a *new* way of thinking about relationships with your boss that emphasises empathy, understanding, and communication.

Are you ready to take control of your work relationships and create a more positive and fulfilling work experience? Keep reading to discover actionable steps you can take to build stronger connections with your boss.

How do I deal with a difficult boss?

Managing difficult bosses can be intimidating, but there are strategies you can employ. These include setting clear boundaries, practising assertive communication, seeking feedback from colleagues, and considering reporting the behaviour to HR.

How can I manage stress at work?

Managing stress at work necessitates several strategies. These include practising good self-care habits like getting enough sleep, exercising regularly, and eating healthily; setting boundaries around work tasks; prioritising tasks; and seeking assistance from colleagues or a mental health professional if needed.

How can I manage my emotions at work?

To manage your feelings at the office, try techniques like deep breathing, mindfulness meditation, cognitive restructuring (CBT), and seeking support from colleagues or a mental health professional. Practise good self-care habits and set boundaries around work time.

How should I handle conflict with my boss?

Establishing effective communication and being willing to compromise are the keys. Try listening actively, identify common goals, and focus on finding solutions rather than blame. If the conflict persists, consider seeking support from a mediator or HR.

How can I improve my relationship with my boss?
Building trust and communication are the keys to improving your relationship with your boss. Make sure to set clear expectations, request feedback and be proactive in all you do. Be respectful yet professional as well, while striving to find common ground.

Types of bosses

Here are some types of bosses you might come across in the workplace, along with real-world scenarios and strategies for dealing with them effectively:

The micromanager:
This type of boss wants to be involved in every aspect of your work, which can feel stifling and frustrating. They may ask for regular updates on progress, question every decision you make, or redo your work according to their liking.

Manage this type of boss effectively:
Outlining clear expectations with your boss will help them understand what success looks like and when they can trust you to work independently. This will allow both of you to stay on track.

Let your boss know when you require support, guidance, or feedback. Doing this will enable them to recognise when it is appropriate for them to become involved in your work and when it is not.

Keep your boss informed of your progress and let them know when tasks have been completed. Doing this will help build trust and showcase your competence.

The Absentee boss:

Your boss may often be absent or disengaged, making it difficult to receive feedback or direction. They might not respond to emails promptly, cancel meetings at the last minute, or provide clear goals and objectives.

Manage this type of boss effectively:
Make a list of tasks you want your manager to complete each day to keep them focused.

Seek feedback from colleagues or mentors, rather than waiting for your boss to provide direction or guidance.

Take ownership of getting feedback by scheduling regular check-ins with your manager to discuss progress and any challenges encountered.

Be specific in outlining what support you need from your boss in order to succeed in your role. This way, both of you are on the same page.

The Bully:
This type of boss can be aggressive and intimidating, making it difficult to work effectively. They might yell at you in front of colleagues, make unreasonable demands, or belittle you.

Manage this type of boss effectively:
Stay calm and focused. Don't let your their behaviour overwhelm you. Remain composed, focused on your work. Use CBT techniques to rationalise your thinking. Don't immediately react. This could land you in hot water.

Establish boundaries and stand up for yourself through assertive communication. Let your boss know that their behaviour is unacceptable, and that you expect them to treat you with respect.

If the situation becomes untenable, consider reporting it to HR for support and advice on how best to handle it. They have the expertise necessary to provide help and solutions.

Consider another job if this behaviour continues.

The Perfectionist:
This boss has high standards and can be difficult to please. Your supervisor might scrutinise every detail of your work, require long hours, or be overly critical of mistakes.

Manage this type of boss effectively:
Communicate your own goals and objectives with your boss. Being honest about your aspirations will enable them to gain insight into what drives you and what matters most to you. This will allow them to gain a better understanding of where you stand on issues important to you.

Managing stress in the workplace

Here are some tips for managing stress at work, along with practical actionable steps and encouraging words:

Identify your stressors: Begin by recognising what exactly is causing you stress at work. Is it a particular task, an employee conflict, or something else entirely? Once identified, you can begin crafting strategies to manage these stressors effectively.

Practise self-care: Taking care of yourself is key for managing stress. Make sure you get enough sleep, eat nutritiously, exercise regularly and take breaks throughout the day to recharge.

Prioritise tasks: Create a to-do list and prioritise items according to urgency and importance. Doing this can help you stay organised and reduce stress levels.

Communicate with your boss: If your workload is causing stress, talk to your boss about it. Be clear about your needs and suggest possible solutions.

Seek support: Reach out to a trusted colleague, mentor, or friend about your stress. Sometimes just talking about it can help ease some of the tension.

Things to Say:
"I'm feeling overwhelmed right now. Can we discuss my workload and see if there's any way we can prioritise tasks?"

"I need to take a break and recharge. I'll be back at work in 15 minutes."

"I'm feeling overwhelmed with this project. Can we come up with some solutions together?"

"I'm feeling a lot of pressure right now. Can we set up a meeting to go over expectations and goals?"

"I'm feeling anxious about this meeting. Can we take a few minutes before to review the agenda?"

Navigating power dynamics in the workplace

Navigating power dynamics in the workplace can be a complex and emotional experience. These include how power is distributed between individuals or groups within an organisation as well as how that power is exercised during day-to-day interactions.

Power dynamics that are out of balance can lead to feelings of frustration, anxiety, and stress. To manage these emotions in such circumstances, it's essential that you are self-aware, honest about what you are bringing to the table, and take specific actions to address the power dynamics at play.

Setting clear boundaries, communicating assertively, seeking support from colleagues or mentors, and practising self-care are all ways you can regain control over your emotions when faced with power dynamics.

Doing so may result in improved relationships with co-workers, increased job satisfaction levels, and an overall more positive work environment.

How to do this:

Identify triggers: Pay attention to any situations or people that cause you an intense emotional response. Stop before you react. By being aware of these triggers, you can better prepare and manage your emotions more efficiently.

Try thinking:

"What situation or person am I feeling this way about?"

"What emotions am I experiencing, and how intensely?"

"What physical sensations am I sensing in my body as a result of these feelings?"

Practise self-awareness: Take time to reflect on your emotions and reactions in different scenarios, so that you can recognise patterns and areas for growth. This will help you gain clarity around what needs improving or changing in yourself.

Use assertive communication: When dealing with colleagues or superiors, use assertive communication techniques. This involves outlining your needs and opinions clearly and respectfully without being aggressive or passive in your approach.

Try this:

"Thank you for your feedback, but I need more specific examples to understand how I can improve."

"I understand that you have a lot on your plate, but give me clear direction on my tasks so I can ensure I'm meeting expectations."

"I'm uncomfortable with your language and approach. Can we please have a respectful, productive conversation?"

Seek feedback: Seek feedback from colleagues and superiors on how you can improve and develop. Doing this can help build stronger relationships and boost your performance.

Use problem-solving techniques: When faced with a challenging circumstance, use problem-solving methods to identify potential solutions and carefully weigh the pros and cons of each. Doing this will enable you to approach the situation more objectively and manage your emotions more effectively.

Try this:

To yourself: *"Let's take a step back and consider this logically. What are some potential solutions to this problem? What are the pros and cons of each option? How can I approach this situation more objectively?"*

To your boss: *"I understand there's an issue we need to tackle. Let's take a moment to brainstorm potential solutions and weigh the benefits and drawbacks of each option."*

"Doing this will help us approach this situation more objectively and come up with a solution that benefits everyone involved."

Building emotional resilience: Foster your emotional resilience by practising self-compassion, using positive self-talk, and celebrating your strengths and successes.

Focus on solutions, not blame: When faced with a challenge or conflict, try to find solutions instead of assigning blame. Doing this can help you approach the situation more constructively and manage your emotions more efficiently. It can also help you manage your emotions by shifting your mindset from a reactive state to one of proactive problem-solving.

By finding solutions, you are taking control of the situation and actively working towards resolution rather than getting stuck in an endless cycle of anger, frustration, or blame. Doing this helps you feel more empowered and confident in handling it yourself, which reduces feelings of stress or anxiety. Approaching it constructively reduces chances for saying or doing something you may regret later which further helps manage emotions more positively.

Some examples of how to focus on solutions instead of blame:

Take a step back and assess the situation objectively. Ask yourself what the issue is and what potential solutions could address it. Remove the emotion altogether.

Avoid assigning blame or assigning responsibility. Instead, focus on pinpointing the underlying issue and working together with others to find a resolution.

When discussing an issue, use *"I"* statements rather than *"You always cause us to miss deadlines."* Instead, say, *"I feel frustrated when a deadline is missed."*

Brainstorm potential solutions with your team or colleagues. Encourage everyone to contribute and consider all ideas, even those that seem unconventional.

Evaluate each potential solution based on its feasibility, cost, and impact. Consider both short- and long-term consequences before making a final decision.

Communication techniques for handling conflicts with superiors

Communication techniques for handling conflicts with superiors refer to specific strategies and approaches individuals can use to address disagreements that arise with their bosses or managers. These tactics help individuals feel empowered and confident when handling difficult conversations, leading to a more positive work environment.

By effectively communicating and resolving disagreements, individuals will build stronger relationships with their superiors and experience greater job satisfaction and happiness.

How can effective communication help foster stronger connections with superiors?

Effective communication can help build trust and understanding between you and your superiors. By openly discussing and resolving conflicts, it shows them you are invested in the team's success and willing to work collaboratively towards shared objectives.

How to do this:

Make time to meet with your boss to discuss your current workload and any worries or queries you may have. Use active listening techniques to fully comprehend their perspective and respectfully reply.

Example: *"Hello [Boss], I was hoping to arrange a meeting with you to review my workload and determine how we can collaborate to ensure I meet expectations. What date and time works best for both of us?"*

Use *"I"* statements when discussing issues or expressing your opinions. Doing so helps to avoid blame or accusatory language and promotes a more productive conversation.

Example: *"I am feeling overwhelmed with my current workload and would appreciate some guidance on prioritising tasks. Can we discuss how to ensure I meet expectations while still managing a manageable workload?"*

Can communication skills really improve job satisfaction and happiness?

Absolutely. Communication is vital for creating healthy workplace relationships. When disagreements are handled effectively and feedback is given with respect, employees feel valued, appreciated, and content in their job.

How can I improve my communication skills with my superiors?

Practise active listening, which involves paying full attention to what the other person says without interrupting or planning a response. Also, use *"I"* statements instead of accusatory or blaming language when expressing needs and opinions.

Finally, be open to receiving feedback and having difficult conversations when necessary.

Exploring the impact of emotions on your relationships with co-workers

In today's workplace, it's almost impossible to avoid interacting with co-workers. Forming positive relationships is essential for creating a productive and healthy workplace environment. Conflicts and misunderstandings among co-workers can lead to negative emotions and a stressful work atmosphere. In this next part, we'll cover techniques for cultivating healthy relationships with your colleagues, managing disputes effectively, and collaborating effectively.

We will also examine the significance of communication and its influence on individual and team success. By mastering these skills and applying them in real-world scenarios, you can foster a more productive work atmosphere.

How does a positive work culture impact emotions?

A supportive work culture can foster feelings of community and belonging among employees, leading to greater job satisfaction and happiness. It fosters open communication, collaboration, and an overall sense of purpose at work.

What are some ways to foster a positive work culture?

To foster such an atmosphere, employers can promote team-building activities, recognise and appreciate employee contributions, encourage open communication, and prioritise employee wellbeing. Employees too can contribute by showing support to colleagues, demonstrating empathy, and exuding positivity.

Try these:

Start a gratitude journal: Before leaving work each day, write down three things you are thankful for. Doing this can help focus your mind on the positive aspects of your job and foster an upbeat outlook.

Take breaks in nature: Studies have shown that spending time outdoors can reduce stress levels and enhance moods. Take a short walk during your break at work in an adjacent park or nature reserve for some fresh air and some peaceful reflection.

Organise a team volunteer day: Initiate a day where your colleagues and you can give back to an important cause together. This can create an atmosphere of camaraderie between colleagues and help foster relationships outside of work.

Create a positive message board: Set up a message board in a common area where employees can post positive quotes, messages or accomplishments to encourage positivity and foster an encouraging work environment. This will help spread positivity throughout your workplace.

How can I manage my emotions in a negative work culture?

Navigating an environment of toxic work can be challenging. To stay sane, take care of yourself by practising self-care and seeking support from trusted colleagues or a mental health professional. Focusing on the positive aspects of your job, setting boundaries, and communicating needs and concerns with employers or HR departments are all effective strategies for managing emotions.

Try these:

Create a positive work bubble: Surround yourself with positive colleagues and create an atmosphere of positivity at work. Plan social events, engage in stimulating conversations, and focus on solutions instead of problems.

Find meaning in your work: Strive to find purpose and meaning in the tasks you undertake, even if they seem daunting. Doing this will keep you motivated and focused on the bigger picture.

Set achievable goals: Setting achievable goals can give you a sense of control and accomplishment in an otherwise stressful work environment. Doing so may boost your self-esteem and reduce stress levels significantly.

If a project involves multiple deliverables, create an organised plan with specific deadlines for each component. Celebrate each task's completion to boost morale and motivation. Doing this can give you greater control over your workload while decreasing stress levels.

Explore new opportunities: If your current work environment is consistently negative and toxic, consider seeking new opportunities that align with your values and goals. Doing this can give you a sense of control and renewed optimism about your career prospects.

If writing is your passion, consider starting a blog or exploring freelance writing opportunities in your free time. Not only will this provide a creative outlet and an inspiring sense of achievement, but it may also lead to new career prospects within the field that interests you. By exploring these new options, you are taking control of your career while improving your emotional wellbeing by doing something that brings joy and fulfilment.

What are the advantages of a positive work culture?

A supportive work culture can foster employee satisfaction, boost productivity levels, reduce turnover rates, and enhance employee retention. It also fosters feelings of purpose and pride within the workplace, that ultimately will cause greater job fulfilment and happiness for everyone involved.

How can I manage my emotions when dealing with difficult co-workers?

Practise empathy and active listening, set boundaries, and maintain a professional demeanour.

How can I address conflicts with my co-workers productively?

Use assertive communication, focus on finding solutions instead of blaming or criticising, and seek mediation if necessary.

How can I foster a meaningful relationship with a co-worker who I don't get along with?

Find common ground and shared interests, express appreciation for their contributions, and maintain respectful communication.

How can I manage my emotions when receiving criticism or negative feedback from a co-worker?

Take a step back and objectively assess the feedback; avoid taking it personally and use it constructively to enhance your work.

How can I manage a co-worker who is always negative or toxic?

Create boundaries and limit interactions as much as possible, maintain an effective professional demeanour and seek support from your manager or HR department, depending on the severity of the issue.

Here are some examples of questions you could use CBT to ask yourself when dealing with a negative or toxic co-worker:

"What evidence do I have that this co-worker is always negative or toxic?"

"Are there any instances when they have been positive or helpful?"

"What other explanations could there be for their behaviour?"

"Could there be personal issues outside the workplace affecting their mood?"

"How can I frame their behaviour in a more positive light?"

"Can I view it as an opportunity for patience and empathy, or an opportunity for assertiveness and boundary setting?"

"How have I dealt with similar situations in the past?"

"Which strategies proved successful or ineffective?"

"What can I do to take care of myself and manage my emotions in this situation?"

"How can I focus on the positive aspects of my job and interactions with co-workers, instead of allowing one negative person to bring me down?"

Techniques for handling conflicts with co-workers

Conflicts with co-workers can be incredibly stressful and emotionally draining. It is often difficult to navigate these situations without feeling overwhelmed, frustrated, or angry. Overreacting or being unprofessional can have serious repercussions, such as damaged relationships, decreased productivity, and even job loss. That's why having effective techniques for handling conflicts at the office is so essential. By remaining calm, using assertive communication, and focusing on finding solutions, you can foster a positive work atmosphere and build stronger relationships with colleagues.

Strategies for resolving conflicts between co-workers

Identify the issue: Define clearly and objectively the problem at hand, including its root cause.

Show empathy: Actively listen to what your co-worker has to say without interrupting or becoming defensive. Remember, it may not be about you.

Express yourself calmly: Express your own perspective in a respectful and calm tone, using "I" statements.

Try these:

"I find it frustrating when you interrupt me during meetings. Can we create a system to prevent interruptions and ensure everyone has an opportunity to speak?"

"I appreciate your input, but I disagree with the direction you are taking this project. Can we explore other options and come up with a compromise that works for both of us?"

"I feel disrespected when you ignore my emails and requests for information. Can we create a communication plan and ensure we respond to each other promptly?"

"I find it offensive when you use offensive language in the workplace. Can we please be mindful of our language and maintain a professional atmosphere?"

"My ideas seem to be dismissed without consideration. Can we take time to discuss them and provide constructive criticism?"

Maintain a calm and respectful tone when speaking, and avoid using accusatory or blaming language. By sharing your own perspective and feelings, you can spark a productive dialogue that moves towards resolution.

Find common ground: Look for areas of agreement and build on those.

Collaborate on solutions: Brainstorm solutions together and work together towards reaching an outcome.

Set boundaries: Make sure your boundaries and expectations are understood by everyone in order to avoid future conflicts.

Try these:

Here are some real examples of setting boundaries at work:

"I understand you may need assistance with your project, but I have my own workload to take care of. Let's set a specific timeline for when I can be of service."

"I value your opinions, but let's stay on track and avoid getting sidetracked."

"We understand you may feel strongly about this subject, but please refrain from using profanity or speaking disrespectfully."

"I feel uncomfortable discussing personal matters at work. Let's keep our conversations professional during working hours."

Establishing clear boundaries helps you avoid miscommunication and potential conflicts with co-workers.

Focus on the future: Instead of dwelling on past disagreements, strive to move forward and find a resolution.

Take a break: If emotions are running high, take a break and come back to the discussion when both parties are calm and collected.

Following up: Once a resolution has been reached, follow up to ensure the agreement is being adhered to and both parties are satisfied.

Here are some real examples of how you can follow up after resolving a conflict with a co-worker:

Send an email thanking your co-worker: Write a brief email expressing your appreciation for their time and help in resolving the issue. Confirm any agreed-upon actions or next steps, and assure them you will follow up to ensure everything remains on track.

Schedule a meeting: Set up a short meeting to check in with your co-worker and discuss the progress since resolving the conflict. Ask if any additional concerns or issues have arisen since then, and confirm that the solutions agreed upon remain viable options for both of you.

Discuss in person: If your co-worker is located close by or in the same office as you, stop by their workspace and check in. Ask how things have been going and if there have been any issues since you resolved the conflict. Emphasise how important open communication and your willingness to work together are to creating a productive work environment.

Implementing these strategies can encourage open communication, mutual respect, and effective problem-solving among co-workers, creating a more positive work atmosphere and increased job satisfaction for all.

15

How Your Feelings Affect Interactions With Strangers
UNDERSTANDING THE ROLE OF EMOTIONS IN BUILDING CONNECTIONS

In today's fast-paced world, we often find ourselves engaging with strangers daily. From simple conversations with baristas to long conversations with new acquaintances, these encounters shape our perspectives of the world around us. Unfortunately, despite their importance, many struggle with effective communication and creating meaningful relationships with strangers, leading to feelings of isolation, frustration, and missed chances for growth and connection.

In this chapter, we will look at the significance of effective communication and building empathy with strangers. We'll identify common pitfalls and obstacles that may occur during these interactions and offer strategies for overcoming them. Moreover, we'll deep-dive into how self-awareness and personal responsibility play a significant role in cultivating healthy relationships with unfamiliar people.

By mastering these skills and applying them in practical scenarios, you can develop greater assurance and connection when engaging in real-world interactions, opening up new possibilities for personal and professional growth.

We will also cover the significance of social interactions for your emotional well-being. By understanding how communication with strangers affects you, you can take control of your reactions and lead a more satisfying life.

We'll address topics such as managing social anxiety, setting boundaries, and dealing with difficult strangers, providing practical strategies for managing emotions in various scenarios.

If you want to expand your social circle, create deeper connections in your community, or simply feel more confident when engaging with strangers, this chapter has the tools and knowledge you need for success.

The importance of communication in everyday interactions

Here are some questions and answers about communication in everyday interactions with strangers and how to manage them emotionally:

Q. Why is communication essential in everyday interactions?

A. Communication forms the basis of all relationships, whether with friends, family, or strangers. Effective communication allows us to express ourselves clearly, comprehend other perspectives, and create meaningful connections.

Q. How can poor communication negatively impact us emotionally?

A. Poor communication often results in misunderstandings, frustration, and conflict. When our message is not received correctly or someone misinterprets yours, we may feel disrespected, unimportant, or even angry.

Q. How can we effectively communicate with strangers?

A. Active listening, asking open-ended questions, and being aware of our body language are all effective tactics for connecting with new people. Furthermore, approaching conversations with a positive and curious attitude helps build rapport and foster trust.

Q. How can we manage our emotions in everyday interactions?

A. It is essential to recognise our feelings and comprehend how they may be impacting our communication. Practising self-awareness, taking deep breaths, and focusing on the present moment will help us manage these feelings more effectively, so we can communicate more effectively.

Q. How can we prevent misunderstandings in communication with strangers?

A. One way to avoid misinterpretations is by clarifying and confirming our understanding of the message received. This can be done by restating what has been said or asking questions for clarification.

Q. How important is empathy for effective communication with strangers?

A. Empathy is the capacity to understand and share another person's emotions. By approaching conversations from an empathic place, we are better able to form connections and foster meaningful relationships.

Q. What are some common barriers to effective communication with strangers?

A. Common obstacles such as language, cultural differences, and personal biases can hinder our efforts at effective communication with others. By being aware of these issues and striving to overcome them, we can improve how well we connect with strangers.

Q. How can we have difficult conversations with strangers respectfully and productively?

A. It is essential to approach difficult conversations with an open mind and a willingness to listen. Using *"I"* statements, acknowledging the other person's perspective, and searching for common ground can help create a productive and respectful dialogue.

Q. How can we build trust with strangers through communication?

A. Demonstrating honesty, reliability and consistency in our interactions will help build trust with strangers. Likewise, being attentive in conversations, fulfilling commitments made, and listening intently all play a role in building this type of relationship.

Here are some likely emotions experienced when interacting with strangers in common scenarios:

At the shops

When things go smoothly:

- Satisfaction from finding what you need.
- Politeness and friendliness from the cashier.
- Appreciation for excellent service.

On the flip side:

- Frustration or anger if an item is out of stock.
- Impatience if there's a long queue.
- Irritation or annoyance if the cashier is rude or unhelpful.

What you could try instead:

Reframe your thoughts: Instead of getting irritated or annoyed at a rude or unhelpful cashier, try reframing your perspective. Consider that they may be having an especially difficult day or lacking adequate training. By doing this, you can shift your perspective and manage your emotions more effectively.

Using assertive communication: If you feel that your needs aren't being met, use assertive communication to express them. For instance, *"I understand the item is out of stock, but I am disappointed as I specifically came here to buy it. Could there be any way you could let me know when it will be back in stock?"* This way, you can assert your needs while maintaining a respectful tone.

On the road

When things go well:

- Calmness and relaxation if traffic is flowing smoothly.
- Politeness and consideration if other drivers allow you to merge or pass.
- Satisfaction from arriving at your destination on time.

If it doesn't go as planned:

- Anxiety or stress if there is heavy traffic or an accident.
- Anger or frustration when other drivers are reckless or aggressive.
- Impatience or irritation if there is a delay or you are running late.

What you could try instead:

Practise deep breathing. Take a deep inhale and exhale slowly to help relax your body and mind. Focus on your breath as you exhale, trying to release any tension or frustration as you do so.

Listen to relaxing music or a podcast: Tuning into music or podcasts you enjoy can help shift your focus away from the situation and towards something more positive, helping reduce feelings of anxiety, stress, or impatience.

Reframe your thoughts: Instead of dwelling on the negative aspects of a situation, attempt to shift your focus onto something more positive. For instance, instead of becoming angry with other drivers for being reckless or aggressive, remind yourself that only you are in control of your own driving and safety. This can help you feel in control and reduce feelings of anger or frustration.

Did you leave enough time for your journey? Be honest about the part you played.

Think of the entire journey and what you can control. Remember to use CBT techniques for what you can and can't control.

On public transportation

When things go smoothly:

- Relaxation or productivity when reading, listening to music, or working while travelling.
- Gratitude when public transportation arrives on time.
- Politeness and friendliness from other passengers.

When things don't go as planned:

- Frustration or anger if transportation is delayed or cancelled.
- Discomfort or irritation if the vehicle is packed or uncomfortable.
- Anxiety or stress if there's a bumpy ride.

What you could try instead:

Find a distraction: To combat discomfort or irritation when the vehicle is packed or uncomfortable, try finding something else to focus on. This could include listening to music, reading a book, or engaging in an enjoyable activity such as colouring or knitting. Focusing on something else helps take your mind away from any unpleasant feelings you may be experiencing.

Reframe the situation: When feeling anxious or stressed during a bumpy ride, try framing the situation in a more positive light. Rather than dwelling on discomfort or potential danger, focus on enjoying the scenery or the fact that you are on your way to somewhere exciting. Doing this can help shift your perspective and reduce feelings of anxiety.

Think of a backup plan for every journey, just in case. Focus on the solution rather than the blame.

At a social event

The positives:

- Excitement or anticipation of meeting new people if everything goes according to plan.
- Enjoying good conversation and shared interests.
- Satisfaction from making new friends or connections.

The negatives:

- Shyness or nervousness when engaging strangers.
- Boredom or awkwardness if the conversation is tedious or uninteresting.
- Disappointment or frustration when an event fails to deliver on its promises.

What you could try instead:

Shyness when engaging strangers: Take a few deep breaths to relax, remind yourself that feeling shy is normal, and focus on the other person by asking questions and paying attention to their responses. You could also use some icebreaker questions or find common ground to start a conversation with this individual.

Why not try asking these conversational starter questions:

"What brings you to this event?"

"Have you been to this event before?"

"What has been your favourite part of the event so far?"

"Have you met anyone interesting tonight?"

"Do you have any recommendations for things to do in the area?"

"How did you find out about this event?"

"What type of events do you usually attend?"

"Do you have any hobbies or interests that you like to pursue in your free time?"

"What do you like to do for fun?"

"What kind of music do you enjoy listening to?"

Boredom or awkwardness: If the conversation seems tedious or uninteresting, try steering it towards topics that interest you or suggesting a different topic altogether. If that doesn't work, politely excuse yourself and find another activity you enjoy instead.

Disappointment or frustration when an event doesn't live up to your expectations: Try to adjust your expectations and focus on the positive aspects of the experience, even if it wasn't exactly what you expected. If you're really unhappy, consider leaving early or finding ways to make the most of it, such as engaging with those around you or finding a new activity to do.

At restaurants

When things go well:

- Satisfaction from good food and service.
- Experiencing a pleasant experience with the server, allowing you to thank them for this and to show your gratitude and appreciation towards them.

When things don't go as planned:

- Frustration or disappointment if the food is of poor quality or not what you ordered.
- Impatience or irritation when there is a long wait for food or service.
- Anger or annoyance if the server is rude or unhelpful.

You could try this:

Speak up: If the food is of poor quality, is not what you ordered, or you experience poor service, it's essential to address the situation calmly and assertively. Talk politely with the server or manager and explain the situation using *"I"* statements instead of accusatory language; this way, you can take control of the situation and guarantee all your needs are being met.

Here are some ways you can assertively speak up in these scenarios:

If the food is of poor quality or not what you ordered,

"Excuse me, the dish seems overcooked. Could you please replace it?"

"I'm afraid this dish is not what I ordered. Could you please double-check my order and bring me the correct one?"

If you experience poor service or an extended wait:

"We apologise, but we have been waiting for our food for some time now. Could you give us an update on how long it might take?"

"Excuse me, it appears we have been waiting for our server for some time now. Could you please send someone over to assist us?"

"I apologise, it has been a while now and we're getting quite hungry - could you check on the status of our food?"

If the server is rude or unhelpful:

"Excuse me, I appreciate your hard work, but I was hoping for a more friendly service."

"I apologise, but your tone and attitude are not acceptable. Could you please speak to us more politely?"

"I am sorry to report that I am not satisfied with the service we've received. Could you please send over another server or speak to a manager?"

Shift your focus: Instead of dwelling on the negative aspects of your dining experience, try to focus on the positive. Take time to appreciate the ambience or the company of those you are dining with. Additionally, use this time as an opportunity to try new menu items or cuisines and expand your culinary horizons. By shifting your perspective, you will empower yourself to enjoy every moment despite any setbacks that arise during the meal.

In all of these situations, there are many times when things go in our favour, and yes, sometimes they don't. It is important to understand that there is a balance to managing your emotions.

Remember, factually, that things aren't all bad all of the time.

Building empathy and understanding with strangers

Empathy is the capacity to understand and share another person's emotions. It requires us to put ourselves in their shoes and see life from their point of view. Empathy for strangers implies showing compassion and understanding even if we do not know them personally.

By being empathic with someone unfamiliar, you can:

Listen actively: Pay close attention to what the other person is saying and ask follow-up questions to demonstrate your interest in their perspective.

Reflect emotions: Acknowledge the feelings someone else is experiencing, even if you don't share them. For instance, say something like, *"I can understand why you might feel that way,"* or *"That sounds frustrating."*

Show empathy: Try to put yourself in the other person's shoes and imagine how you would react if you were in their situation.

Doing this can help you gain a better understanding of their viewpoint.

Avoid judgement: Don't assume anything or draw hasty conclusions about someone's situation. Instead, approach them with an open mind and attempt to comprehend their perspective.

Empathising with a stranger can help you build an emotional connection, even if it's only for brief moments. Not only does it make them feel heard and valued, but it also boosts your own confidence as you navigate daily interactions with others.

It can help us manage our emotions in several ways. Firstly, it allows us to comprehend and connect with them on an intimate level, leading to feelings of compassion and reducing anger or frustration. By acknowledging that someone may be going through a difficult time, we can lessen our tendency to judge or criticise their behaviour or words and instead provide them with empathy and kindness. Additionally, developing empathy and understanding with strangers can boost our own sense of self-awareness and emotional intelligence, helping us better manage our own emotions in various circumstances. Ultimately, being empathetic towards strangers helps us foster stronger relationships and enhances our overall well-being.

How can you use CBT when interacting with strangers?

CBT can assist individuals in recognising and challenging negative thoughts and beliefs that may be causing them to feel anxious, stressed, or frustrated when interacting with strangers. For instance, someone may hold the belief that all strangers are dangerous or untrustworthy, which may lead them to feel fearful in social settings.

The old saying, *"There is no such thing as strangers, only friends we haven't met yet,"* can be a real help when interacting with unfamiliar people.

It can put a positive spin on our nervous feelings when coming across strangers in any walk of life and can really empower us to deal with these challenging situations with poise and strength. In the real world, which can be a scary place for socially challenged individuals, this can be a game-changer when it comes to making new acquaintances in the workplace or social spaces. Holding the belief that strangers are dangerous and something to be feared, or worse, avoided, can lead to social isolation and feelings of worthlessness.

Through CBT, people can learn how to challenge this belief and replace it with a more rational and realistic one, such as, *"Some strangers may be dangerous, but most people are trustworthy and kind."*

16

Breaking Free From Insecurity
STRATEGIES FOR OVERCOMING ATTACHMENT WORRIES AND BUILDING STRONGER RELATIONSHIPS

This chapter delves into the nuanced world of attachment and its impact on our emotions, particularly within relationships. Although attachment worries are common, many struggle to manage them emotionally. We have to find a way to recognise our role in creating these attachment issues and understand that, while some factors may be within our control, there are others that remain firmly beyond it. To adequately manage these attachment worries, we need to find a way to power forward and come to a point where accepting the reality that we cannot control everything is possible.

Attachment anxieties can have a devastating effect on our mental health, relationships, and overall well-being. Many have tried various approaches to cope with these worries but have experienced little relief. This chapter offers an alternative perspective - a *new* way of understanding attachment styles and how they impact relationships. We will cover strategies for overcoming attachment issues and creating secure attachments, as well as techniques for managing anxiety and stress within these intimate contexts.

By exploring concrete examples and real-world applications, this chapter will show you how to apply these concepts and techniques in your daily life. There will be some actionable steps suggested that you can take to make meaningful progress towards overcoming attachment worries.

By understanding the root cause of these issues and employing the strategies provided here, you will be better equipped to conquer attachment worries and cultivate healthier, more fulfilling relationships.

What exactly is relationship attachment?

Relationship attachment refers to an emotional bond formed between individuals, particularly in close intimate relationships. This bond shapes how we connect and interact with one another for emotional support and comfort.

Attachment theory, developed by John Bowlby, suggests our early experiences with caregivers shape our attachment styles, which then influences how we approach and engage in adult relationships.

There are four primary attachment styles: **secure, anxious, avoidant,** and **fearful-avoidant,** each with its own characteristics, behaviours, and ways of managing emotions within those connections.

How are emotions and attachment related to each other?

Attachment and emotions are intimately connected, as the attachment bond formed within relationships serves as a ground for emotional regulation, support, and security. Our closeness with others profoundly impacts our sense of emotional well-being; therefore, our attachment style plays an integral role in how we manage and express emotions within those intimate connections.

Our early experiences with caregivers shape our attachment style, shaping beliefs about self-worth and trust as well as how we seek comfort from others. These beliefs then shape our adult emotional reactions and behaviours in relationships.

Individuals with **secure attachment** tend to have a healthy balance of emotional expression, autonomy, and trust, which leads to more stable and satisfying connections.

On the other hand, people with **anxious, avoidant,** or **fearful-avoidant attachment** styles may struggle with emotional regulation, communication difficulties, and diminished trust. Ultimately, this will potentially lead to relationship difficulties as well as increased emotional distress.

Here are examples of different attachment styles, how they manifest in real life, the emotions involved, and potential outcomes:

Secure attachment

Everyday behaviour: Individuals with secure attachment feel secure being close to others and relying on them for emotional support. They express their feelings honestly, maintaining an equilibrium between autonomy and emotional intimacy.

Emotions: Trust, comfort, confidence, emotional stability.

Words:

"I trust you."
"I'm here for you."
"We can work through this together."

Consequences: Positive, healthy relationships built on trust, open communication, and mutual support.

Anxious attachment

Everyday behaviour: People with anxious attachments tend to seek validation and assurance from their partners. They may be overly dependent, clingy, jealousy-prone, or insecure.

Emotions: Anxiety, fear of abandonment, neediness, insecurity.

Words:

"Do you still love me?"
"Why didn't you call me?"
"I'm worried you'll leave me."

Consequences: Relationships that become overly needy, lack trust, or struggle with emotional regulation may suffer as a result. This could leave partners feeling overwhelmed or smothered, potentially leading to the breakdown of the relationship.

Avoidant attachment

Everyday behaviour: Individuals with avoidant attachment often struggle to form close emotional connections and appear emotionally distant. They may avoid intimacy, value independence, and struggle to express their emotions openly.

Emotions: Discomfort with vulnerability, fear of closeness, emotional detachment, and self-reliance.

Words:

"I don't need anyone."
"Let's not talk about feelings."
"I'm fine on my own."

Consequences: Shallow or unsatisfying relationships due to emotional distance, poor communication, and difficulty forming deep connections may lead to feelings of loneliness and alienation.

Fearful-avoidant attachment

Everyday behaviour: Individuals with fearful-avoidant attachment often struggle with conflicting desires for intimacy and distance, leading to unpredictable behaviour. They may crave closeness yet fear it, creating turbulent relationships.

Emotions: Fear of abandonment, anxiety, mistrust, and confusion.

Words:

"I want to be close to you, but I'm scared."
"I don't know what I want."
"I can't trust anyone."

Consequences: Relationships that are unstable and inconsistent often display confusion, poor emotional regulation, and difficulty building trust. This may lead to a cycle of push-pull dynamics in which partners feel uncertain and emotionally worn out.

Understanding one's attachment style is essential for managing emotions and behaviours that arise within it, leading to healthier, more fulfilling relationships.

Can you see yourself in any of these attachment styles?

How to overcome attachment issues and build secure attachments

Attachment styles are fundamental to how we interact with others in romantic relationships, impacting communication, trust, and emotional health. By understanding and managing our attachment styles, we can improve both our relationships and our overall happiness.

The following strategies and actionable steps will help you to discover your own personal attachment style so you can foster healthier, more secure connections with your romantic partner.

Positive strategies to cope with attachment styles:

Enhance self-awareness: Recognise and understand your attachment style, and how it influences your thoughts, feelings, and behaviours in relationships. Reflect on past experiences to identify patterns that could have arisen due to this style.

Actionable step: Keep a journal to record your thoughts, emotions, and behaviours during various relationship scenarios. Analyse these entries to recognise patterns and gain a better insight into your attachment style.

Develop effective communication: Work on communicating your feelings, needs, and boundaries openly and honestly with your partner. Doing this will create a safe space for both of you to share any attachment-related issues openly.

Actionable step: Consistently use *"I"* statements when expressing your emotions or needs. For instance, say something like *"I feel worried when we don't talk for a few days,"* rather than saying, *"You never speak to me."*

Cultivate empathy: Enhance your capacity to understand and share the emotions of your partner. Doing so will enable you to respond more sensitively to their needs, creating a deeper emotional bond.

Actionable step: As your partner shares their feelings or experiences, listen attentively and try to put yourself in their shoes. Ask open-ended questions to gain a better insight into their viewpoint.

Try asking:

"Can you tell me more about how that situation made you feel?"

"What was going through your mind when that happened?"

"How do you wish things could have been different in that situation?"

"In what ways did this experience affect your emotions or thoughts?"

"What would you like me to understand about your feelings in this situation?"

"How do you think this experience has influenced your perspective on [the specific topic]?"

"What do you need from me to feel supported in situations like this?"

"Are there any specific actions or changes you'd like to see moving forward?"

"What steps can we take together to address or prevent this from happening again?"

"How can I help you feel more comfortable discussing your emotions and experiences with me?"

Asking the above open-ended questions can help one deal with one's emotions in several ways:

Improved communication: By asking questions and actively listening, you create a safe space for communication that reduces misunderstandings and allows you to express your own emotions more effectively.

Emotional regulation: Gaining empathy for your partner's perspective can help you develop empathy and reduce your own emotional reactivity, making it easier to manage your emotions during conflict or difficult circumstances.

Increased self-awareness: Through these conversations, you gain valuable insights into your own emotions, triggers, and patterns. This self-awareness can equip you with the power to take proactive steps to manage your emotions more effectively in the future.

Strengthened relationship: Open communication and empathy foster trust and emotional intimacy in your relationship. A stronger bond provides a secure platform for managing emotions and feeling more secure within your attachment.

Enhancing problem-solving skills: By understanding your partner's emotions and needs, you can work together to find solutions to problems or challenges you face as a couple. This collaborative approach can give you greater emotional power over yourself and more control over how you handle emotional distress.

Personal growth: Engaging in honest conversations promotes growth both personally and as a couple. As you gain more insight into yourself and your partner, you can develop healthier coping strategies and emotional responses, which will ultimately give you increased empowerment.

Developing self-soothing techniques: Acquiring healthy ways to manage your emotions when feeling anxious or insecure in a relationship will help maintain a balanced emotional state and prevent attachment-related issues from getting out of hand.

Quick questions to sum up attachment and relationships

As we have previously discussed, the notion of *'attachment'* refers to an emotional bond formed between individuals, particularly in romantic relationships. Its roots in early childhood experiences shape how we engage with our partners, express feelings, and manage conflict.

Attachment plays a major role in how we form romantic connections and how we handle emotional turmoil.

Here are some of the most common questions asked about attachments, and their answers to help with your overall understanding of attachment styles and their impact on relationships:

Q: How are attachment and emotions connected?

A. Attachment styles shape how we express and regulate emotions within relationships, leading to different emotional reactions such as feeling secure and comfortable or anxious and fearful, which in turn influences relationship dynamics and overall satisfaction levels.

Q: How do early childhood experiences shape attachment styles?

A: Early experiences, especially those with primary caregivers, shape our attachment styles. Consistent nurturing leads to secure attachment; insecure or inconsistent care may create anxious, avoidant, or fearful-avoidant attachment styles.

Q: Can attachment styles evolve over time?

A: Absolutely! Attachment styles can evolve with self-awareness, therapy, and positive relationship experiences. Establishing a secure attachment with someone supportive or working on personal growth leads to more secure attachment patterns in relationships.

Q: How can I identify my attachment style?

A. Through self-reflection, taking online quizzes, or working with a therapist, you can identify your attachment style. Assessing patterns of behaviour, emotional responses, and relationship history also offers insight into these patterns of attachment.

Try this:

Self-reflection: Take a close look at your past and current relationships, paying special attention to how you typically handle emotional situations, handle conflict, and approach closeness or distance in romantic relationships. Pay attention to any patterns that emerge.

Research: Familiarise yourself with the different attachment styles (secure, anxious, avoidant, and fearful-avoidant) and their characteristics. Compare your behaviour and emotions in relationships to these styles to determine which resonates most with you.

Online quizzes: Various online quizzes can help determine your attachment style through a series of questions about thoughts, feelings and behaviours in relationships. Popular options include the *"Attachment Styles and Close Relationships Inventory and Experiences in Close Relationships"* questionnaire.

Therapy or counselling: Working with a therapist or counsellor can help you explore your attachment patterns in-depth. They will offer an objective assessment of your style and support you throughout the process of comprehending and resolving any attachment-related issues.

Be mindful that people may exhibit traits from multiple attachment styles, and your style may evolve over time as you gain self-awareness and engage in different relationships.

Q: How can I improve my attachment style?

A: To enhance your attachment style, begin by understanding and accepting your patterns. Seek therapy or counselling to address underlying issues, develop emotional regulation skills, and construct a healthy self-image. Embrace open communication, trust, and vulnerability in relationships by choosing partners who are supportive yet understanding.

Q: How do different attachment styles impact relationships?

A. Secure attachment leads to healthy and trusting relationships; insecure attachment styles can create emotional instability, conflict, and dissatisfaction. Recognising and working on your attachment style will improve both relationship dynamics and your mental wellbeing.

Q: Can two people with insecure attachment styles have a successful relationship?

A: Yes, two people with insecure attachment styles can have a successful relationship if both parties commit to self-awareness, growth, and open communication. Addressing attachment issues and developing emotional regulation skills can lead to healthier relationship patterns.

Q: How can I support a partner with an insecure attachment style?

A: Be patient, understanding, and compassionate. Promote open communication, build trust, and offer consistent emotional support. Encourage your partner to seek therapy or counselling if necessary and work together on developing healthier relationship patterns together.

In conclusion, attachment and emotions are closely connected because our attachment style, formed through early experiences, shapes how we experience, manage, and express emotion within relationships.

A **secure** attachment bond provides a stable platform for emotional well-being, while **insecure** attachment styles may lead to emotional difficulties or cause relationship problems in the future.

The secret to a successful relationship is to identify which attachment style both you and your partner have and then work through the advice given in this chapter to forge a pathway through and overcome the obstacles that present themselves throughout your relationship using the actionable steps offered here.

17

The Power Of Forgiveness And Letting Go For Personal Growth And Well-Being

In this insightful chapter, we will explore the transformative power of forgiveness and letting go, emphasising its importance in relationships as well as personal growth. While forgiving someone you've hurt is essential for any healthy relationship, doing so can be one of the most challenging aspects of emotional resilience.

The root of the issue often lies in our tendency to hold onto grievances and past wrongs, either consciously or subconsciously. This could be due to our own shortcomings or those of others. To identify and resolve these emotional obstacles, cultivating self-awareness and honesty are essential skillsets.

Life presents us with elements we can control and others we cannot. Although we may not have control over another's actions, we still have influence over our own reactions, emotions, and choices.

Understanding this distinction is essential to learning to forgive and let go. Holding onto resentment and hurt can have far-reaching effects. Not only does it cause emotional pain, stress, and even physical health problems for us, but it can also create tension in our relationships. Many have tried different strategies to deal with these feelings but found them ineffective or unsustainable.

In this chapter, we'll discover a fresh take on forgiveness, emphasising its significance for building deeper connections and emotional well-being. We'll look at various techniques to cultivate forgiveness and let go of past hurt, giving you the tools needed to create healthier, more rewarding relationships.

By the end of this chapter, you'll have tangible examples and practical applications of how forgiveness and letting go can transform your life, giving you access to emotional liberation and deeper relationships. With these principles in hand, you can begin applying them right away to experience their positive effects in your own life.

Forgiveness – what is it?

Traditional views of forgiveness often focus on pardoning someone else for their mistakes or wrongdoings, but our modern perspective emphasises the significance of self-forgiveness as well. Acknowledging our own shortcomings and errors is a necessary part of forgiveness; by admitting them, we open the door to personal growth and self-compassion.

Furthermore, this new perspective on forgiveness encourages us to view it as an ongoing practice rather than a one-time event. Forgiveness is an active process that necessitates consistency, patience, and mindfulness; it requires cultivating an attitude of understanding and acceptance towards ourselves and others.

Quick questions and answers about forgiveness:

Q: What is forgiveness and why is it essential?

A: Forgiveness is the act of releasing anger, resentment, and the desire for revenge against someone who has wronged you. It's essential because it promotes emotional healing, personal growth, and healthier relationships.

Q: Does forgiveness involve accepting someone else's actions or forgetting what transpired?

A: No. Forgiveness does not imply condoning or forgetting hurtful behaviour. Instead, it involves releasing the negative emotions connected to the event and moving on more healthily.

Q: How does forgiveness affect our emotions?

A: Forgiveness can reduce negative emotions like anger, bitterness, and resentment. It also promotes positive ones like empathy, compassion, and inner peace that contribute to improved emotional well-being.

Q: Will forgiving someone make me feel empowered?

A: Absolutely! Forgiveness can give you control over your emotional responses and release the burden associated with holding onto grudges. It helps you focus on personal growth and healing rather than dwelling on past hurts.

Q: How can I forgive someone who refuses to apologise or acknowledge their wrongdoing?

A: Forgiveness is a personal choice and should be motivated by your emotional well-being rather than the other person's actions. You can still forgive someone even if they don't apologise or acknowledge their wrongdoing. Focus on the positive effects of forgiveness for yourself; remember that you are releasing negative emotions for your own benefit, not that of another.

Q: Does forgiveness always lead to reconciliation?

A: Forgiveness and reconciliation are distinct processes. While forgiveness is a personal decision, reconciliation requires both parties to work together to rebuild trust and repair the relationship. While forgiveness can be an important first step, successful reconciliation requires both parties' willingness and effort to address what caused the conflict for it to be addressed.

Q: How can I practise forgiveness in my daily life?

A: Cultivate empathy and understanding, practise self-compassion, and draw upon the lessons learned from difficult experiences. Regularly assess your emotional state, acknowledge any lingering resentment, and work on forgiving those feelings through forgiveness. You can also utilise mindfulness techniques or journaling to process emotions more effectively and maintain a forgiving mindset.

How to forgive somebody - and yourself

Forgiving someone who has wronged or hurt you can be difficult, but it is necessary for your emotional well-being and the health of your relationships.

Here are some steps that will help you truly forgive someone:

Acknowledge your emotions: Acknowledge and validate any emotions you're feeling as a result of someone else's actions. It is essential to accept these feelings rather than suppress or deny them.

Empathise with the other person: Try to understand the situation from their point of view. What was the underlying reason they wronged you or behaved the way they did? Were they angry, scared, or worried about something? Consider their intentions, background, and potential reasons for their behaviour. This doesn't guarantee you will agree with them, but it can help you put things into a broader perspective.

Express your feelings: If it is appropriate and safe, express your emotions to the person who hurt you. Use *"I"* statements to explain how their actions affected you without blaming or attacking them. Doing this can provide a sense of closure and allow you to move forward with confidence.

Decide to forgive: Make the decision to forgive and let go of resentment and anger. Remember that forgiveness is a choice and more about your emotional well-being than the other person's actions.

Reframe your thoughts: Switch your focus from the negative aspects of the situation to the lessons learned and personal growth that emerged as a result. Doing this can help you cultivate a more optimistic mindset and prevent negative emotions from taking control.

Practise self-compassion: Acknowledge that everyone makes mistakes, including you. No one is perfect, and forgiving those who fall short of our expectations can be cathartic. Show yourself kindness and understanding as you work through the process of forgiveness.

Let go of expectations: Recognise that forgiveness does not necessitate forgetting or that your relationship will return to its former state. Instead, view forgiveness as an opportunity to release negative emotions and move forward.

Rebuild trust (if appropriate): If the relationship is worth maintaining, work on rebuilding trust and setting healthy boundaries. This may take time and effort from both parties involved.

Remember, forgiveness is a process, and it may take some time to fully let go of the negative emotions attached to an experience. Be patient with yourself and practise forgiveness regularly to promote emotional healing and personal growth.

What if I still feel anger?

Dealing with anger when someone has wronged you and refuses to apologise can be a thorny issue.

Here are some strategies for managing your rage and finding inner peace:

Acknowledge your feelings: Acknowledge and accept that you are feeling angry. Suppressing these emotions can lead to increased resentment, with potentially negative repercussions for both mental and physical well-being.

Give yourself time and space: Give yourself some space to process your emotions. It is essential to give yourself this space rather than try to force yourself to feel better right away.

Engage in healthy coping mechanisms: Find healthy ways to cope with your anger, such as exercising, doing deep breathing exercises, or practising mindfulness meditation. Avoid unhealthy coping mechanisms like substance abuse or lashing out at others. Remember: STOP. Don't automatically react.

Seek support from friends, family, or a therapist: Expressing your emotions to someone you trust can help you process them and gain new perspectives on the situation.

Reframe your thoughts: Rather than dwelling on the other person's refusal to apologise, try to focus on what you can learn from this experience and how it has allowed you to grow as a person. Remember, you are only responsible for your own emotions and reactions to an issue or situation.

Establish boundaries: If the person who wronged you is still part of your life, set boundaries to protect yourself from further emotional harm. You do not have to spend time with these people or be around them if they are a negative influence on you. This may be a difficult decision and may involve restricting contact or setting clear expectations for future interactions.

Focus on what you can control: While you cannot influence another person's decisions or get them to apologise, you do have the power to manage your own emotions and responses in the face of adversity. Focus on managing yourself instead. Managing your emotions and reactions during such times will give you insight into the situation more effectively.

Practise forgiveness: Forgiveness should be for your own emotional well-being, not that of the other person. Work on letting go of anger and resentment, even if they don't apologise. Remember that forgiveness is a process that may take some time.

Accept that not everyone will apologise: Recognise that some people may never apologise or acknowledge their wrongdoing. Accepting this fact can help you let go of your anger and move on with your life.

Remember, you are on your own journey through life. If the people you come across in life are not as far down the forgiveness track as you are, it is ok. They will get there in their own time. Focus on yourself and what you can control. This is the true path to happiness and fulfilment in life.

18

Overcoming Jealousy And Cultivating Emotional Resilience

Jealousy, an emotion born out of fear and insecurity, can have devastating effects on our personal and professional relationships.

This chapter examines the causes, science behind, and consequences of jealousy while offering practical strategies and a fresh outlook to enable you to confront jealousy head-on and cultivate healthier, more secure connections.

Understanding jealousy - Origins and science

Jealousy is a complex emotion with roots in both neurological and evolutionary mechanisms. From a neurological perspective, jealousy activates areas in the brain responsible for processing social information, emotional regulation, and threat perception, such as the amygdala, prefrontal cortex, and anterior cingulate cortex.

Evolutionarily speaking, jealousy has been suggested to have a beneficial role in maintaining reproductive success and resource protection. In romantic relationships, jealousy can arise from a perceived threat of losing one's partner to a rival, which historically may have had consequences for reproductive success and survival.

By understanding the neurological and evolutionary bases of jealousy, we can better appreciate its powerful impact on our thoughts, emotions, and behaviours, as well as devise more effective strategies for managing it effectively.

Strategies to manage jealousy:

Effectively managing jealousy requires self-awareness and understanding the underlying factors responsible for this emotion.

Here are some strategies to help manage jealousy and foster healthier relationships:

Reflect on your emotions: Take time to identify and comprehend the source of your jealousy. Are you feeling insecure, threatened, or inadequate? Understanding these emotions will enable you to address them more effectively.

Communicate openly: Discuss your feelings with your significant other in a non-confrontational way, allowing for an honest dialogue about concerns and emotions. Clear communication helps prevent misunderstandings and builds trust.

Foster self-esteem: Work on building your self-worth by acknowledging and celebrating your strengths, successes, and personal development. A strong sense of worth can reduce feelings of insecurity that often fuel jealousy.

Building self-esteem takes dedication and hard work. Here are some practical steps you can take to increase your self-worth:

Create achievable objectives: Break larger objectives down into smaller, achievable steps. As you complete each one, you'll feel a sense of accomplishment, which will boost your self-esteem.

Practise self-compassion: Show yourself the same kindness and understanding you would extend to a friend. Acknowledge that nobody is perfect, so it's okay to make mistakes. Learn from them and move forward.

Surround yourself with positive energy: Cherish those relationships and environments that lift you up and encourage you. Avoid toxic relationships and environments that could bring you down or lead you to doubt your worth.

Challenge negative self-talk: When negative thoughts about yourself arise, challenge their validity and replace them with more optimistic assessments of your abilities and strengths.

Engage in activities you enjoy: Doing things that you are passionate about can help boost your self-esteem by giving you a sense of competence and satisfaction with your accomplishments.

Develop new skills: As you acquire new abilities or refine existing ones, developing them can increase your self-assurance as you become increasingly capable.

Practise self-care: Prioritise your physical, emotional, and mental well-being by regularly exercising, eating a balanced diet, getting enough sleep, and seeking professional assistance when necessary.

Keep a success journal: Keep track of your accomplishments, compliments received, and personal growth moments in an inspirational journal. Reading this journal regularly can serve as a reminder of your capabilities and progress.

Affirmations: Use positive affirmations to boost your self-worth and overcome negative self-perceptions. Write down or say statements like *"I am capable,"* *"I deserve love,"* or *"I am strong,"* and use them as motivation when facing down negative thoughts or perceptions about yourself.

Practise trust: Trust is the cornerstone of any healthy relationship, so it's essential to give your partner the benefit of the doubt. Remind yourself why you trust them, and work on strengthening that bond by being reliable and trustworthy yourself.

By employing these strategies, you can take control of your jealousy and build stronger, more secure connections with your partner while experiencing emotional well-being and personal growth.

Everyday manifestations of jealousy

Jealousy can take many forms in our daily lives, from words and actions to the consequences of those decisions. Someone experiencing jealousy may become overly possessive, constantly checking their partner's phone or social media accounts and demanding to know their whereabouts at all times. They might express their jealousy through passive-aggressive remarks or hostile behaviour towards their partner or perceived rivals.

These manifestations of jealousy can have devastating consequences, such as emotional distress and erosion of trust within a relationship, potentially leading to estrangement or even physical distance between partners. By understanding its everyday signs and taking proactive measures to address it before it causes irreparable harm to our relationships, we can learn to recognise jealousy when it is present and take appropriate measures before it causes irreparable harm.

With self-awareness, you can recognise your triggers and thought patterns, and accept responsibility for any role in the development of jealousy.

By understanding jealousy and its effect on relationships, implementing effective strategies to manage it, and appreciating its potential for personal growth and empowerment, you can conquer this challenging emotion and lay a stronger foundation for your relationships.

19

Developing Effective Coping Strategies For Loss And Bereavement

Grief is an intense and complex emotion that we all must confront at some point in our lives. Whether it's the loss of a loved one, a relationship, a pet, or even a treasured dream, grieving can be an arduous journey filled with challenges and hardships.

It's often said that *"grief is the price we pay for love,"* and anyone who has lost a loved one, especially in tragic circumstances, will attest to this saying. The hole that losing a loved one leaves behind is one that can never be filled and will be felt for the rest of a person's life. Even losing a pet can trigger a specific grieving process, that can be felt on as deeper level as losing a loved human member of the family or a close friend.

Grieving is a natural process that helps us come to terms with loss and find healing. In this chapter, we'll look into the science of grief, answer common questions about it, and provide strategies for managing and empowering ourselves in our relationships.

By understanding grief's various effects on us, we can better prepare to manage it and move forward in a positive light. This chapter offers key takeaways as well as practical steps that we can take to support ourselves and others during this difficult time. By the end, you will feel empowered and equipped to navigate grief with strength and resilience.

Grief can take many forms and look different for each individual. However, some common signs of grief include:

- Feelings of intense sadness, anger, guilt, shock or numbness.
- Alterations in sleep patterns, appetite or energy levels.
- Withdrawal from social activities and relationships.
- Struggles with motivation and focus.
- Physical symptoms, such as headaches, fatigue or weight changes.

It's common for people to experience an outburst of emotions during the grieving process. This could include crying, yelling, or acting out in anger. Outbursts are a natural part of grieving and can be used as an outlet to release pent-up emotions. But we must remain mindful of how our actions may impact others and seek support if needed.

It is essential to remember that everyone grieves differently, and there is no single path through this process. If you or someone you know is struggling with grief, reach out for support from loved ones, mental health professionals, or grief support groups. With time, understanding, and self-care, most people can work through their sorrow and find healing.

Questions and answers about grief

Q: How do I know if I'm grieving properly?

A. There is no standard way to grieve, as everyone's experience is unique. Common feelings and behaviours during grief include sadness, anger, guilt, shock, and numbness. You must allow yourself to experience these feelings rather than suppress or ignore them.

Q: How do I cope with the intense emotions associated with grief?

A: You can manage intense emotions by taking care of yourself, reaching out to loved ones for support, and seeking professional assistance if necessary. Engaging in self-care activities such as exercise, mindfulness, or relaxation techniques may also be beneficial.

Q: How can I support someone grieving?

A. Listen attentively, validate their feelings, and offer practical assistance as needed. Avoid offering unsolicited advice such as telling them to *"move on"* or *"get over it."* Respect their grieving process and be patient throughout this period of transition.

Q: How can I cope with the loss of a loved one while still taking care of myself?

A: It is essential to take care of yourself during this trying time. Make time for self-care activities like exercising, spending time with loved ones and engaging in hobbies. It may also be beneficial to seek support from friends, family or a mental health professional if needed.

Q: How do I talk to children about grief and loss?

A. When speaking with children about grief and loss, be honest, straightforward and age-appropriate. Give them space to express their feelings and answer their questions as best you can. Reassure them that they're not alone in feeling sad or grieving for a loved one.

Q: How can I manage the grieving process while still maintaining relationships with others?

A: Grieving can put a strain on relationships, so it's essential to communicate openly with loved ones and enlist their support. Let them know what you need from them and make time for self-care, as well as seek professional mental health guidance if needed. Additionally, taking care of oneself is important; make time for it and reach out if any mental health professionals are necessary.

Q: How can one cope with grief?

A: Some helpful strategies include practising self-care, reaching out to loved ones for support, journaling, and seeking professional assistance if needed. Additionally, engaging in physical activity, practising mindfulness, and finding meaning through your loss can all be beneficial.

Q: How do I handle holidays and special occasions after a loss?

Holidays and other important dates after a loss can be difficult. To cope, take care of yourself and reach out for support from loved ones. You may create new traditions or find other ways to honour your loved one's memory.

Q: How long does grief last, and is there a timetable for healing?

A: Grief has no set duration; however, with time, support, and self-care it becomes less intense and easier to manage.

Remember, everyone's grief journey is unique, and there is no single path to take. Be kind to yourself and seek support when needed.

You could try finding some kind of meaning in your loss. Try reflecting on ways to honour the memory of those you've lost, such as volunteering, starting a new tradition, or writing about your experience.

The science behind grieving

Grief is an intense emotional response to loss that can have physical and psychological repercussions. Studies have revealed that grief activates similar areas of the brain as physical pain, leading to intense feelings of overwhelm.

Grief releases chemicals like cortisol and adrenaline into our system, which may manifest physically as fatigue, headaches, or changes in appetite.

Studies have also demonstrated that grieving can have a significant effect on our mental health, leading to symptoms of depression and anxiety.

Grieving also alters behaviour; it may cause us to withdraw from social activities, struggle with motivation and focus, and experience changes in sleep patterns.

However, it's essential to note that grief is not a disorder or mental illness but an entirely natural and healthy reaction to loss.

What you could do today:

Create a memorial garden: Plant flowers or plant a tree in honour of your loved one and visit it regularly as an outlet to stay connected to their memory.

Create a memory jar: Fill a jar with items that remind you of your loved one, such as photos, trinkets, or notes. You can add to it over time and revisit it whenever you feel connected to their memory.

Write a letter: Express your feelings and thoughts by writing a letter to someone special in your life. You can keep it for yourself or send it on to someone who would find it meaningful.

Try expressive arts therapy: Use activities such as painting, drawing, or sculpting to express your emotions and process grief.

Participate in a symbolic ritual: Construct an act that expresses your love and connection to someone special, such as lighting a candle or releasing balloons.

Whatever way you overcome grief, remember that with every passing day, it will get more bearable to deal with. It won't ever go away—the feeling of loss—but you will learn a way of dealing with it as time goes on. It is incredibly important to accept that you feel the way you do; never deny your feelings, excuse them, or diminish their importance. Accept this new normal and treasure the time you had with your departed loved one.

20

Healing From Trauma
MANAGING EMOTIONS AND BUILDING RESILIENCE IN THE FACE OF ADVERSITY

Trauma is an intensely distressing or disturbing experience that can have a lasting effect on someone's mental and emotional well-being. It can result from physical or sexual abuse, natural disasters, war, or car accidents, leaving victims feeling overwhelmed, anxious, and disconnected from others.

In this chapter, we'll investigate the science behind trauma as well as its emotional triggers, answer common questions about it, and offer practical strategies for managing it effectively in the aftermath. By better understanding trauma, we can better prepare to manage it and move forward in a positive light.

An emotional outburst from trauma can manifest in various forms and differ for each individual. Common signs of such a reaction may include:

Crying: Sudden and intense crying spells may indicate an emotional outburst due to trauma.

Yelling or shouting: Yelling or shouting may be indicative of an emotional outburst caused by trauma.

Acting out in anger: Excessive anger, such as throwing objects or breaking things, may be indicative of an emotional outburst from trauma.

Withdrawal: Withdrawing from social situations or isolating oneself can be indicative of an emotional outburst from trauma.

Physically expressing anger: Physical displays of anger, such as hitting or breaking objects, may indicate an emotional outburst from trauma.

Disruptive behaviours: Engaging in disruptive or impulsive behaviours, such as substance abuse or recklessness, may be indicative of an emotional outburst from trauma.

It's essential to remember that everyone responds differently to trauma, and these signs may not be present in all cases. If you or someone you know is dealing with an emotional outburst from trauma, reach out for support from loved ones, mental health professionals, or support groups.

Most common questions about trauma

Q: What is trauma?

A: Trauma is an intensely distressing or disturbing experience that can have a significant impact on one's mental and emotional well-being.

Q: What are some common symptoms of trauma?

A: Common manifestations can include anxiety, depression, irritability, difficulty sleeping, and feelings of guilt or shame.

Q: How does trauma impact relationships?

A: Trauma can wreak havoc on relationships and make it hard to maintain contact with others. To combat this, communicate openly with loved ones and seek professional assistance if needed from mental health professionals.

Q: How long does it take to recover from trauma?

A: Recovery times vary between individuals, but with adequate time and support as well as self-care, many people can begin healing and moving forward.

Understanding Trauma

Trauma is an intense emotional reaction to a deeply distressing or disturbing experience. It can have both physical and psychological repercussions on one's well-being, including changes to brain structure and function. Trauma also causes stress hormones like cortisol or adrenaline to be released, which may manifest physically as headaches, fatigue, or changes in appetite.

Trauma can cause physical and psychological symptoms, such as changes to the brain structure and function, the release of stress hormones, and symptoms of anxiety, depression, and PTSD.

Additionally, trauma strains relationships by making it difficult to form meaningful connections with others.

Recovery from trauma requires time and is unique for each individual, but with support, self-care, and therapy, most people can find healing and move forward.

Things you can try to cope with trauma:

Create a vision board: Compose an array of images, quotes and symbols that represent your goals and aspirations. Doing this can help you stay focused on the future while giving you control over your life.

Alternative therapies: Alternative treatments such as acupuncture, massage or aromatherapy can be an effective way to manage stress and anxiety.

Write a letter to your trauma: Crafting a letter to your trauma can be an effective therapeutic method for processing emotions and finding closure. It may help you express all of your feelings and thoughts in writing.

Engage in expressive arts therapy: Try activities such as painting, drawing, or sculpting as a means to express your emotions and process trauma.

Participate in a ritual: Create an act of healing and resilience by lighting a candle or releasing biodegradable balloons.

Try a new hobby: Discover an enjoyable hobby like gardening, cooking, or photography as a way to focus your energy and find meaning in life.

Connect with nature: Spending time outdoors, such as hiking, camping, or gardening can be a calming and grounding experience.

21

Breaking The Grip Of Depression
STRATEGIES FOR MANAGING EMOTIONS AND OVERCOMING THE CHALLENGES OF MENTAL ILLNESS

Depression is a debilitating mental health condition that affects millions of people around the world. It's believed to be caused by a combination of biological, genetic, environmental, and psychological factors and can lead to feelings of sadness, hopelessness, and even a loss of interest in life.

In this chapter, we'll investigate depression's science behind it, answer common questions about it, and offer practical strategies for managing it effectively in both personal and professional relationships.

By better understanding depression, we can better prepare ourselves to manage it effectively and move forward in a positive light.

Did you know?

Depression can take different forms for different

people: From persistent feelings of sadness to physical symptoms like fatigue, headaches, and changes in appetite.

Depression and inflammation are connected: Studies have demonstrated that chronic inflammation may increase the likelihood of depression and other mental health conditions.

Depression and creativity often go hand in hand: Many creatives, such as writers, artists, and musicians have reported experiencing depression while using their art for therapy.

Depression can affect memory: Depression may lead to memory problems, such as difficulties recalling and retaining information.

Depression may run in families: Genetics plays an important role in the likelihood of developing the disorder.

Exercise can be as effective as medication for treating depression: Studies have demonstrated that regular exercise can be just as successful at treating depression as medication and has long-lasting effects.

Depression has been linked to other physical health problems: Depression has been known to increase the likelihood of heart disease, diabetes, and chronic pain; making it harder for individuals to manage these conditions effectively.

Depression can manifest itself in many different ways and forms for different individuals. Some common signs of depression may include:

- Feelings of sadness, hopelessness, and worthlessness.
- Loss of interest in life, hobbies, and activities.

- Alterations in sleep patterns, such as insomnia or excessive sleeping.
- Modifications to appetite and weight.
- Loss of energy and motivation.
- Difficulty concentrating or making decisions.

It is essential to remember that everyone experiences depression differently, and these signs may not be present in all cases. If you or someone you know is struggling with depression, reach out for support from loved ones, mental health professionals, or support groups. With time, understanding, and self-care, most people can work through their issues and find healing.

Summary questions about depression

Q: What is depression?

A: Depression is a widespread mental health condition that affects millions of people worldwide. Symptoms include feelings of sadness, hopelessness and an overall loss of interest in life.

Q: What causes depression?

A: Depression can be caused by a combination of biological, genetic, environmental and psychological factors.

Q: How does depression impact relationships?

A: Depression can put a strain on relationships and make it difficult to maintain meaningful connections with others. To combat this, communicate openly with loved ones and seek professional assistance if needed from mental health professionals.

Q: How long does it take to recover from depression?

A: Recovery times differ for each individual, but with enough time and support as well as self-care many people can begin healing and moving forward.

Discovering depression's scientific basis

Depression is a multifactorial mental health condition that impacts both the mind and body. Studies have demonstrated that depression can alter brain structure and function to affect mood, behaviour, and cognition.

Depression also releases stress hormones like cortisol, leading to physical symptoms like headaches, fatigue, and changes in appetite. Furthermore, depression has an adverse effect on relationships; making it difficult to maintain meaningful connections with others.

Recovering from depression requires time and the support of loved ones; however, with self-care, therapy, and these resources, most people can find healing and move forward with their lives.

Things you can try to combat depression:

Incorporate mindfulness into your life: Practises such as meditation, deep breathing, or yoga can reduce stress and promote relaxation.

Stay active: Exercise has been proven to be a useful tool in managing symptoms of depression. Make time for physical activity in your daily life, even if it's just taking a short walk.

Connect with others: Fostering healthy social connections is essential for managing depression. Surround yourself with supportive friends and family, or consider joining a support group or therapy session.

Write in a journal: Journaling can be an effective therapeutic tool for managing feelings and thoughts associated with depression.

Exploring creative outlets: Use creative activities such as painting, drawing, or writing to express emotions and process feelings related to depression.

However you combat depression, try and remember that nothing is forever, and with a targeted plan for tackling your depression, you can and will find a way through your dark feelings and make it through to better days. Exploring the ideas in this chapter will give you a solid start on the pathway to recovery.

The rest of your life starts today.

22

Exploring The A-Z Of Emotions
UNDERSTANDING THE COMPLEXITY AND DIVERSITY OF HUMAN FEELINGS

A - Anger: A strong feeling of displeasure or hostility that is often caused by perceived wrongdoing, frustration, or injustice. Manage anger by deep breathing, counting to ten, and using *"I"* statements to express your emotions.

B - Boredom: A feeling of dissatisfaction that stems from a lack of engagement or interest. Combat boredom by engaging in activities that challenge and stimulate you, as well as discovering new hobbies or interests.

C - Compassion: Demonstrate empathy and understanding for the suffering of others by practising active listening, volunteering, and honing your empathy skills.

D - Disappointment: An intense feeling of sadness or frustration due to unmet expectations or disappointing outcomes. Manage disappointment by altering your expectations, focusing on what you can control, and seeking emotional support from others.

E - Envy: A feeling of discontent or covetousness regarding another person's possessions, accomplishments, or qualities. Overcome envy through practising gratitude, working on self-improvement projects, and celebrating the successes of others.

F - Fear: An intense emotion caused by a perceived threat or danger. Manage fear by recognising its source, taking steps to reduce it, and using relaxation techniques to soothe your nerves.

G - Gratitude: A sense of gratitude and appreciation for what you have or have experienced. Foster gratitude by keeping a gratitude journal, expressing thanks to others, and practising mindfulness.

H - Happiness: A state of contentment, joy, and satisfaction. Foster your happiness by engaging in activities you enjoy, cultivating meaningful relationships, and focusing on personal growth.

I - Insecurity: Feelings of uncertainty or self-doubt that often stem from low self-esteem. Combat this feeling by building self-confidence, practising self-compassion, and seeking support from others.

J - Jealousy: An emotion caused by a perceived threat to one's valued relationship. To manage jealousy, cultivate trust, boost self-worth, and communicate openly with your significant other, learn to accept who you are as a person and manage this emotion together.

K - Kindness: Demonstrating kindness through genuine concern, generosity, and consideration. Foster this trait by practising empathy, volunteering your time, and performing random acts of goodwill.

L - Loneliness: Feelings of sadness or loneliness due to a lack of companionship or social connections. Combat loneliness by reaching out to friends and family, joining clubs or groups, and partaking in hobbies that interest you.

M - Mindfulness: The practice of being fully present in the moment and fully engaged with your thoughts, emotions, and experiences. Develop mindfulness through meditation, deep breathing exercises, and focusing on your senses.

N - Nostalgia: An intense yearning for the past, often accompanied by mixed emotions. Celebrate nostalgia by reminiscing with friends, journaling about your experiences in the past, and finding a healthy balance between the past and present.

O - Optimism: A disposition to look on the bright side and anticipate positive outcomes. Encourage optimism by focusing on the positives, setting achievable goals, and practising gratitude.

P - Pride: An intense sense of satisfaction and accomplishment that arises from one's accomplishments or qualities. Maintain a healthy sense of pride by acknowledging your achievements while remaining humble and eager to learn from others.

Q - Quit: Knowing when to leave a situation that doesn't serve you anymore. Quitting is not failure. It is acknowledging that there is a better path out there for you to follow and recognising that the current situation is not making you happy. Manage your guilt over quitting something by reflecting on the experience, learning from it, and vowing to make better choices in the future.

R - Resentment: An intense feeling of bitterness or indignation caused by perceived unfair treatment or injury. Overcome resentment by practising forgiveness, acknowledging the source of your emotions, and seeking support.

S - Sadness: An overwhelming sense of sadness or unhappiness that may be brought on by loss, disappointment, or other circumstances. Deal with sadness by expressing your emotions, seeking support, and prioritising self-care activities.

T - Trust: Have faith in someone's dependability, honesty, or competence. Demonstrate trust by being consistent, open, and reliable in your actions and communications with others.

U - Understanding: The capacity to comprehend and empathise with the thoughts, feelings, and perspectives of others. Foster this understanding through active listening, asking questions, and being open-minded.

V - Validation: Acknowledging and affirming someone else's emotions and experiences is essential to validating them. Demonstrate empathy by empathising with others, expressing understanding, and avoiding judgement.

W - Worry: An intense feeling of anxiety or unease about an uncertain outcome or situation. Manage worry by recognising its source, taking steps to address it, and using relaxation techniques to soothe your mind.

X - Xenophobia: An irrational fear or dislike of people from different countries or cultures. Overcome xenophobia by educating yourself, engaging in open dialogue, and accepting diversity.

Y - Yearning: An intense desire or longing for something, often accompanied by feelings of sadness or loss. Address yearning by setting goals, working towards fulfilling your needs, and finding healthy ways to cope with unfulfilled desires.

Z - Zeal: An intense drive or enthusiasm in pursuit of a goal or objective. Foster this energy by setting meaningful objectives, maintaining an upbeat outlook, and surrounding yourself with supportive individuals who share your enthusiasm.

By understanding and managing emotions, you can enhance your mental well-being, cultivate healthier relationships, and feel empowered in everyday life. Remember that emotions are an inherent part of being human - learning how to manage them effectively is a lifelong journey that must be undertaken.

Afterword

In conclusion, mastering emotions in relationships is a crucial aspect of creating healthy and rewarding connections with others. As you progress on the road towards emotional mastery, you will become better equipped to tackle any complications or difficulties that come your way.

By applying the strategies and insights provided throughout this guide, you will now begin to experience dramatic improvements in your life. Your newfound emotional intelligence will enable you to build stronger connections with family, friends, and colleagues, leading to more satisfying and fulfilling connections.

As you continue to cultivate your emotional well-being, remember that growth is an ongoing journey. Continue honing skills such as self-awareness, communication, empathy, and conflict resolution while also striving for balance and self-care in your life.

Above all else, remember to be patient with yourself and others. Emotional mastery requires time, dedication, and perseverance. Continue seeking support from loved ones, professionals, and self-

Afterword

improvement materials throughout your journey to make it more successful.

Take advantage of this unique chance to transform your relationships and create the life you desire. By developing emotional intelligence, you will unlock the full potential of those with whom you connect, guaranteeing a future filled with love, understanding, and contentment.

Thank you for taking the time to read this book. I truly hope you have found it inspiring and you now feel empowered to take on the world and all it has to throw at you.

Remember, today is the first day of the rest of your life.

Go out, feel empowered, and achieve everything you've ever wished to.

www.ingramcontent.com/pod-product-compliance
Lightning Source LLC
Chambersburg PA
CBHW050238120526
44590CB00016B/2145